Jacques Lipchitz

The Paris Years

Sculpture and Drawings
1911-1932

October 17–November 23, 2019

Marlborough

THE PARIS YEARS

Jacques Lipchitz (1891-1973) was a key figure of the 20th century art scene, along with major artists like Constantin Brancusi, Pablo Picasso, Julio González, and Alberto Giacometti. They were Lipchitz's contemporaries during the first two decades of the century, sharing interests and projects, and laying the groundwork for a Cubist vocabulary in painting and sculpture. For him, Cubism was a gateway to not as much a style as a philosophy of looking at space, which he could then manipulate in his own way. Lipchitz met Picasso through Diego Rivera in 1914, and in 1915 he met Juan Gris. It was in 1914 when he created his first cubist piece, *Sailor With Guitar*, although he had made earlier cubist drawings. Amedeo Modigliani made a portrait of him and his first wife in 1916 (Art Institute of Chicago).

Throughout the 20th century, Lipchitz's oeuvre attracted international attention from top art scholars and the most prestigious museum directors. His work is represented in almost all of the major museums of the world, including the Museum of Modern Art, Metropolitan Museum of Art in New York, the Israel Museum in Jerusalem, the Tate Gallery in London, and the Museum of Rotterdam. His public works can be seen in cities such as Philadelphia, Rome, Paris, London, Los Angeles, to name just a few.

This exhibit spans those years in Paris, from his arrival in 1909 as a young Jew from Lithuania coming to what was at the time the art capital of the world, through 1933 when the political scene in Europe was moving toward extremes like Nazi national socialism and Soviet communism

Lipchitz's sculpture praxis went through a variety of phases during these years, all of them significant, with a seminal influence on subsequent 20th century sculpture. This exhibit covers the following phases:

1. The early pieces that the young Lipchitz made in France, influenced by French *fin de siècle* sculpture, but with very personal artistry.
2. The early totemic pieces, with a strong sense of volume and mass, 1915
3. The early Cubist pieces, 1913 to 1923
4. The works he called "*transparents*", 1925-1927
5. The use of negative space to shape sculpture, 1929-1931
6. Empty heads, 1932

After this exploratory period, in 1932 Lipchitz began to make a large number of maquettes for public monuments. His seminal work was *Prometheus Strangling the Vulture,* which appeared in the Science Pavilion at the 1937 World's Fair in Paris. It was the kind of public work that he would later develop in exile, mainly in the United States.

Jacques Lipchitz in his studio, ca. 1920-25.

Early Sculpture in Paris, 1909-1913

Lipchitz arrived in Paris in 1909 and attended the École des Beaux-Arts as a guest in classes with Jean-Antoine Injalbert. Injalbert was the sculptor of the statue of Mirabeau in the Pantheon, which Rodin's Victor Hugo, though rejected, had been commissioned to accompany. He also studied at the Académie Julian and Academie Colarosi. He met other artists and the writer Pierre Reverdy (1889-1960) at the Bateau-Lavoir on rue Ravignan in Montmartre and at La Ruche in Montparnasse. He rounded out his education with visits to the Louvre and contemporary art galleries around the city. He was especially interested in non-European art and began to collect it. One example was a carved and painted wooden bowl from the African kingdom of Dahomey.

In this exhibition, *Woman and Gazelles,* (1911) and *Pregnant Woman,* (1912) are representative of this period. The first piece was undoubtedly the bronze version of one of the four plaster pieces shown at the Salon d'Automne (November 15, 1913 through January 15, 1914) at the Grand Palais in Paris: a "*groupe en plâtre*" [plaster grouping] (as were *Femme et Gazelles* [Woman with Gazelles] (maquette for the bronze), *La Baigneuse,* [The bather] *Portrait de Mmlle S* [Portrait of Ms. S.], and *Tête de Jeune Fille* [Head of a Young Girl]). He sold a bronze casting of part of a study for this grouping to the Baron of Gunzburg. His work was beginning to attract praise, including from sculptor Auguste Rodin. Art critic Hilton Kramer would later write: "From the earliest works in the exhibit, the elegant *Woman and Gazelles* (1911-12), we know we are in the presence of a master. But in this period of his artistic development, Lipchitz was a master more in synch with tradition and his regular visits to the Louvre than with the radical innovations of the Modernists. This changed abruptly, however, with his immersion in Cubism and his awakening to African sculpture, and *from here on Lipchitz took up a position on the frontlines of the European avant-garde."* [1]

The Early Totemic Pieces, 1915

In 1913 Lipchitz befriended Mexican painter Diego Rivera (1886-1957), who painted him in the Cubist style, as did Amedeo Modigliani (1884-1920). Rivera also introduced him to Pablo Picasso (1881-1973). At first, Lipchitz didn't take to Cubism. He was particularly unimpressed with Picasso's sculpture, although he and Picasso would later become close friends. In 1914 Lipchitz met writer Jules Romain (1885-1972). Romain gave him some indirect advice on how to make sculpture that was less crystalized, "maintaining a sense of organic life." This resulted in the 1916 sculpture *Head*. Modigliani had finished his limestone piece *Caryatid* (now at MoMA), which was bought in 1919 by architect Pierre Chareau (Bordeaux 1883 - New York 1950), designer of the famous *Maison de Verre* (1927-31). Chareau and his wife Dollie (Louise Dyte) remained devoted supporters of Lipchitz his entire life. He took him to see the sets he designed for filmmaker Marcel L'Herbier, including for *L'inhumaine* in 1924 and *Le Vertige* in 1927, and in 1926 he bought *Femme avec Guitare* from him (now housed at the Hirshhorn). Chareau left Paris for New York in 1939. He then moved to East Hampton, where he built Robert Motherwell's studio out of sections of Quonset huts in 1947. It was Chareau who welcomed the exiled Lipchitz when he arrived in New York in 1941.

These were Lipchitz's influences when he made his wooden sculptures known a *"demountables"* in 1915. He would later destroy most of them. The drawing *La Serveuse* (1915) in this exhibition is an example of this period. After destroying nearly all of these wooden pieces, Lipchitz started work on a series of totems that displayed certain Cubist elements such as blocks of stone, resembling large scale architecture as in *Sculpture* and *Seated Figure* (1915) and *Standing Figure* (1916). Lipchitz was aware that the history of Western sculpture had been closely linked to the idea of the obelisk since antiquity. Whether carved, molded, or cast, over the centuries statues had been conceived as solid monoliths, substantial and autonomous entities—positive objects that to some extent or another exerted their power and weight in space. *Sculpture* and *Seated Figure* are like architectural totems. In terms of mass and volume, they bear a clear resemblance the work of his studio mate at the time, Constantin Brancusi. They inspired writer Waldemar George to describe them as "architectural forms...organisms created...with a sense of composition, with measure and balance that give them the appearance of small monument-style buildings."[2] Two stone pieces from 1915, *Standing Figure* and *Seated Figure* at Jeanne Boucher's gallery, were bought by viscount Charles de Noailles. The two pieces appeared in a 1924 article by Jean Badovic called "*Sculptures architecturales*" [Architectural Sculptures] in the magazine *L'Architecture vivante.*[3]

Poet Paul Dermée also noted the architectural nature of these works: "Jacques Lipchitz is one of the few present-day artists guided by the constructive spirit...the compass and the ruler, those sublime tools of the architect and the mason, were his first toys. Does this explain the architectonic nature of his work?"[4]

Cubist Sculpture, 1913-1925

A young Lipchitz arrived in Paris at the height of a period of revolutionary upheaval in painting, whether at the hands of the Fauves like Derain and Matisse, or the Cubists like Picasso and Braque. He was not drawn to any of them. However, after traveling to Spain with Diego Rivera and other Hispanic artists, he began making some Cubist drawings and sketches. One example was the excellent pencil drawing *Spanish Woman With a Fan* (1913), along with a 1914 pencil and colored chalk drawing. We can compare those to the stony rigidity of another excellent drawing, *Woman in Profile* (1910), which was more closely aligned with the work of his friend Modigliani.

Cubism allowed for a perception of three-dimensional space, a perception that wasn't the product of perspective, but rather of the overlapping and dislocation of planes and geometric coordinates, fusing perspectives and ideas about movement and time. This new geometry of Cubism transferred to the picture plane, to the canvas as a surface, *re-presented* events as they unfold in consciousness, blending situations and consecutive viewpoints. Thus the images in the painting did not represent spatial depth, but rather a rhythm of shapes—a fusion of points of view in search of a new spatial reality. In this sense, Cubism is based on or functions within that same space as other inquiries of the time, such as a mathematical topology tied to a relativist physics, that is, the mixture of David Hilbert's mathematical formalism with Einstein's relativity. For Lipchitz, "Cubism is like standing at a certain point on a mountain and looking around. If you go higher, things will look different; if you go lower, again they will look different. It is a point of view."[5]

We can see two periods in Lipchitz's Cubist phase. The first was "high Cubism" or "synthetic Cubism" which focused on *Commedia dell'Arte* figures like the Harlequins and Bathers, and the other was a more analytical period as seen in the musical instrument reliefs.

In 1922 Lipchitz met American art patron Albert Barnes

Modigliani, Amedeo (1884-1920), *Jacques and Berthe Lipchitz*, 1916. oil on canvas, 32 x 21 3/8 in., 81.3 x 54.3 cm
The Art Institute of Chicago / Art Resource, NY

(1872-1951), who requested his help to purchase works of art for his new foundation located in Merion, Pennsylvania. Barnes commissioned him to make five reliefs. In 1923 the Fine Arts Academy in Pennsylvania exhibited 75 of Barnes's acquisitions in April and May, including seven of Lipchitz's sculptures. In a letter to Barnes written in October while he was at work on the fifth relief, Lipchitz gave the following definition of sculpture: "I consider a sculpture to be complete when it consists of three fundamentals: the philosophical basis, the visual basis, and the representative basis. Any work of art that fails to follow this rule cannot achieve wholeness. Because the philosophical basis is our moral sustenance, the visual basis nourishes our senses, and the representation is the doorway through which, with the visual, we arrive at the philosophy of the work, its Esthetics, if you prefer... It follows from what I said above that the representation is, I believe, a necessary basis but not the most important one... It is so true that everything is subject to the philosophy that this is the only way we can explain the different forms of imagery in different eras and different peoples." In March 1925, the Barnes Foundation opened in Merion.

With the money that Barnes paid him, the sculptor was able to hire architect Le Corbusier to design a residence/studio for him. Le Corbusier, in a letter to the sculptor on December 7, 1922, wrote: "You are one of the few artists who fill me with the desire to possess... Lipchitz, my friend, my taste for architecture makes me lean strongly towards your sculpture, and I find true joy in it. I hope to have the pleasure of working with you one day."[6]

At the end of 1924 Lipchitz went to live in his new home. *La Bagneuse* [Bather] was exhibited in 1925 at the International Exhibition of Modern Decorative and Industrial Arts, outside of the *Pavillon de l'Esprit Nouveau*, which was designed by Le Corbusier and his cousin Pierre Jeanneret. Inside the building, *Marin a la guitare* was exhibited on a landing, which stood out for the time. The renowned architect Pierre Chareau also owned a number of works by Lipchitz at his home at 54 rue Nollet in Paris, such as the 1924 terracotta piece *Seated Bather.* He also commissioned a relief by Lipchitz for his *Cabinet de Travail* at the above-mentioned International Exhibition of Modern Decorative and Industrial in 1925. It is worth noting that three of the greatest architects of the time were Lipchitz's admirers, collectors, and friends: Robert Mallet-Stevens (1886-1945), the aforementioned Pierre Chareau (1883-1950), and Le Corbusier (1887-1965). The brothers Gustave and Auguste Perret (1874-1954) were also admirers, with the latter purchasing a piece in 1922.

This period of Cubist works, widely represented in this exhibition, especially the reliefs associated with the Barnes Foundation, ended when Lipchitz started working on the so-called *transparents,* creating *Joie de vivre,* a monumental work, over seven feet tall, that depicted a dancing figure with a guitar. On February 5, 1928, Jean Prouvè cast the sculpture as a single piece, mounting it on a motorized circular pedestal that took four minutes to revolve full-circle.[7] It was installed at the end of February in Hyeres, in the house built by Mallet-Stevens. The sculptor Brancusi, vacationing in Nice, was there.[8] In the sculptor's words: "it is open, like the *transparents*, despite it being a monumental piece, over seven feet tall. The figure turns on an axis like my first Cubist works, to create its own three dimensional space among the massive forms that interpenetrate from every angle of view so that space flows through the sculpture."[9] In my essay "Art and Nature and Transformations in Sculpture: New Vision of Territory and Landscape,"[10] I state that early 20th century sculpture broke with traditional notions of space with a new kind of space that was more of a question than an answer—a new way of asking oneself, of questioning oneself, of probing the very nature of space—*physical space as relational space.*

The *transparents* and *Joie de vivre* liberated Lipchitz from the language of Cubism. When Lipchitz exhibited his plasters in his first retrospective, *100 sculptures de Jacques Lipchitz* at the Galerie Renaissance in Paris, he displayed the following text alongside the sculpture: "I love the movement of lines". It paraphrases a verse from Charles Baudelaire's *Les Fleurs du mal* (1864) from the sonnet *"La Beauté"*: *"Je suis belle, ô mortels!, comme un rève de pierre (...) Je hais le mouvement qui déplace les lignes (...)Mes yeux, mes larges yeux aux clartés éternelles!"* [I am fair, O mortals! like a dream carved in stone, I hate movement for it displaces lines, My eyes, my large, wide eyes of eternal brightness!]

We can assume that sharing concerns with Pablo Picasso and Juan Gris in Paris in the early decades of the 20th century lay the foundation for Lipchitz's Cubist vocabulary in sculpture, which would later lead to his own personal language, his own spatial music. With his *works*, Lipchitz not only forged new paths with the concept of the interrelation of space and emptiness, he also paved the way for experimentation, for self-reflection in the very praxis of sculpture.

The *"Transparents"*, 1925-1927

Lipchitz made another major contribution to 20th century sculpture in his small individual pieces that he called the *transparents*. In the *transparents*, the imagination completes and closes the image. Planes are not planes as such, but rather membranes that communicate the space between them, as is visible in *Pierrot* (1925), or in *Harlequin with accordion* (1926).

These works are key in that they clear the path for new ways of thinking about the very practice of sculpture and also of painting, as the artist Picabia's works would also do in 1927-28. Picabia's *Transparencies* were exhibited in Paris at the Galerie Theophile Briant in October of 1928. Film critic Gaston Ravel considered them *"sur-impressionism"*, referring to the simultaneity of the overlapping images in film which create the impression of a third dimension without the help of perspective, "a third dimension without the aid of perspective," as artist Marcel Duchamp described it. They were made earlier in the summer of 1927, which Picabia spent with Olga Mohler (1905-2002), his son's Swiss governess and the person with whom he saw the romantic frescoes of Cataluña.

Lipchitz's *transparents* are small pieces, ranging from about 20 to 43 cm, but they are seminal pieces, created as part of a research process: sketches for larger, more important public works. The first *transparents* appeared between last Cubist *Bagneuse*—at two meters tall, the largest one, started after a trip to Lithuania in 1923 and finished in 1925—and two large open air works, *Joy of Life* (1927) and *Song of the Vowels* (1932). All but one of these works were unique pieces cast in bronze, and many of them were housed early on in museums (the Hirschhorn Museum in Washington D.C., Art Gallery in Ontario, Smith College Museum of Art in Northampton, Indiana University Museum of Art in Bloomington, Harvard University Museum of Art in Cambridge, Kunsthaus in Zurich, the Peggy Guggenheim Museum in Venice, et al.).

In his autobiography *My Life in Sculpture,*[11] Lipchitz relates that the body of work he calls the *transparents* was born in early 1925 while he was attending a conference held by a German critic at the Sorbonne. The conference, a part of a series of events organized by the doctor Rene Allendy at the *Societé des étude philosophiques et scientifiques de la Sorbonne* [a study group organized by Allendy devoted to the study of novelties in science and humanities] was given by Paul Westheim (1886-1963). If it had been given by Carl Einstein, Lipchitz would likely have remembered his name because of their mutual appreciation for African art. He was in fact so bored that his mind wandered, and he began to think about his sculptures, leaving early to return to his house where he was working the entire evening making compositions out of scraps of cardboard.

These pieces have the look of forged iron, but they are actually cast, though unique. In the sculptor's own words: "all of these pieces were extremely quick in execution. I normally made them in a day or two, continually excited by the feeling that I had embarked on a whole new pattern of expression [...] These *transparents*, which came upon me with no warning, were a fantastic experience. I had been working for the past several years toward a form of expression continually more solid and monumental. Suddenly, I found myself playing with space, with a kind of open, lyrical construction that was a revelation to me. I have no idea how I came to this. It simply happened; but it was an ecstatic experience. I felt as though I were discovering an entirely new concept of sculpture as space, of the ethereal soul of the sculpture rather than its physical corporeality."[12]

In 1925, two pieces made with very different approaches somehow embody this new concept of sculpture which distances itself from Cubist visual ideas: *Man Leaning on Elbows* and *Musical Instruments*. This melancholy thinker, almost an abstraction, is a departure from Cubist principles. It is crafted like architectural calligraphy, like a flow that is *co-sculpted* by its volume and the void that the figure creates with its sculptural contortions, just as *Joie de Vivre* will later do on a different scale. The depth of his focus is articulated by just three masses, the head and the hands, but the intensity is concentrated or "constructed" in the empty space.

The second piece that challenges the Cubist construction of the great *Baigneuse* is *Woman with guitar* (1925). Earlier pieces, such as the various reliefs of *Musical Instruments* (1923), also do so. In Lipchitz's own words: "the idea of openness was further explored in a different manner in *Musical Instruments*, a free-standing sculpture that emerged from some of the reliefs of musical instruments created in 1923 [...] but it is Cubism with a difference, extremely free, open, interpenetrated, and dynamic."[13] This same tension of interpenetration is what Lipchitz was after in his *transparents*. Lipchitz distanced himself from the principles or the axioms of Cubism in search of greater simplicity, and he distanced himself from Juan Gris's thinking "Cubism is not a manner but an aesthetic, and even a state of mind."[14] Lipchitz attempted to distance himself from this closed aesthetic, and his hands, his "thinking hands", led him from working directly with casting to the experience of the *transparents*. The inter-spaces of these small pieces became a kind of attempt at a new direction, transcending Cubism's exploration of simultaneity and overlapping, and the relationship between space and time.

These ideas of opening the mass in Cubist sculpture, introducing relational space and hollow or negative space, which appears in *Man Leaning on Elbows*, lead to his discovery of his own path manifested in the *transparents*. By casting directly with dry materials like cardboard and wire and using wax to hold it together, Lipchitz was able to get away from the wetness of the plaster and clay to create pieces that offered him greater freedom of visual thought.

It was not just this juxtaposition but also this oscillation of forms that inspired Christopher Green's comparison between Lipchitz's *transparents* and the constructive way Picasso's *Guitar* was made in 1924: "The guitar strings are bars through which we look; and the concertina plane of the fret-board, which has slipped down from the guitar arm above, forces us to look around *behind* it into the caged void. There is less that oscillation between inside and outside which was to be so marked in Lipchitz's *transparents*, more an invitation to penetrate a space which has been shut away from us; closed in, at least partially.'"[15] As Alan Wilkinson has said, Lipchitz also influenced Spain's great sculptors: "Lipchitz's '*transparents*' were among the most innovative works of his career, and they influenced Picasso and Julio González's metal constructions of 1928."[16]

Jacques Lipchitz in his studio at 54 Rue Montparnasse, Paris, ca. 1922.

The *transparents* represented a direction in Lipchitz's way of thinking about sculpture that was free (outside of formal constraints) and spontaneous (outside of technical constraints). They would go on to open many different paths, ways to examine continuity and discontinuity, materiality and immateriality, gravity and anti-gravity, interior and exterior, empty space and hollow space, all fundamental themes in 20th century sculpture. Lipchitz displayed the *transparents*' three-dimensionality in an ambiguous and flattened way, with planes superimposed upon each other as if in interplay of amorphous densities. This way, transparency is transformed by the interplay of planes to create a different volume, not constructed so much as a complex column as with his Cubist sculptures, but in an open space, where the reflectivity of the gaze is open to suggestion. If the motto of Edmund Husserl's phenomenology was "to the thing itself", as was the case with the paintings of Cezanne, Lipchitz's was directly "to the casting!!!" The resulting immediacy of the sculptor's task was that the work of art was not only the thing that is seen (its volume or mass) but is also what is read, a hermeneutics of what is seen (a game of transparencies).

The Introduction of Negative Space, 1929-1931

At the same time that Lipchitz was making the *transparents*, he was working on some pieces where that transparency, as I mentioned earlier, had been replaced by a void, by empty space or negative space. This can be seen in *Man Leaning on Elbows* (1925), the *Reclining Figure* (1929), the *Head of a Woman* (1930) or *Meditation* (1931).

With his *Man Leaning on Elbows* (1925) and above all with *Reclining Figure* (1929), Lipchitz showed us that the sculptor carves not only the space of the stone but also its emptiness; that he also models both mass and void. *Reclining Figure* (1929) is in a way based on simplicity, on the elimination of the rhetorical excesses of the image. Lipchitz draws attention to the shape of spaces and the orchestration of the unspoken. The void becomes a kind of positive sign, rather than a negative one, contrary to tendencies in Western thought when it comes to the void or darkness. Now the void is given dimension by as yet uncreated spaces, it is a "living void", like the silence that occurs between chords, having nothing to do with regular silence: it is an alert silence, a living silence.

If the mystical poet looks for a way to express the ineffable, to build his silence with words, Lipchitz sought to sculpt the void itself, his own void, not the volume of physical mass. The object of sculpture is no longer static, no longer the physical mass of an object placed in space; it is the invigoration of spaces or even the creation of spaces, or the *un-occupying* of them, turning traditional visual explorations inside out. The philosophy of Lao-Tse also examined this idea of the void in the "Tao te Ching" (XI):

> Thirty spokes are joined together in a wheel,
> but it is the center hole
> that allows the wheel to function.
> We mold clay into a pot,
> but it is the emptiness inside
> that makes the vessel useful.
> We fashion wood for a house,
> but it is the emptiness inside
> that makes it livable.
> We work with the substantial,
> but the emptiness is what we use.

This example of the empty space within a pitcher or a jug and the notion of this empty space as something positive is also clearly expressed in philosopher Martin Heidegger's *Die Kunst und der Raum* [Art and Space] in 1968:

> And what would become of the emptiness of space? Too often it only appears as an absence. The void exists as the absence of something to fill it, as intermediate and hollow space.
> Without a doubt, emptiness is more aptly considered a part of the place, therefore it is not absence but rather something to reveal. Language can once again offer us some guidelines. The verb 'lesen' (to gather) is present in the verb 'leeren' (to empty) in its original meaning of 'to gather', what is missing in the place.
> To empty the glass means to gather it, i.e. having found its place, it becomes free.
> To empty the fruits gathered in a basket means to give them place.
> Emptiness is not nothing. Nor is it absence. In visual manifestation emptiness plays the part of a foundational step in the creation of places.

With those pieces, Lipchitz was attempting to shape both internal and external space, their secret connections or shared attributes, not their opposing ones—those points in common, the places where they brush up against each other—places of connection, communion, impact, of vibration between the inner and the outer, the void and mass. A pair of drawings from 1926, *Woman and Guitar* and *Study for Transparent,* help to explain this exploration of overlapping planes and formal rhythms that had led him to create those sculptures mentioned earlier, like *Meditation* or *Musical Instrument*s. Line loses its figurative function, its role as an element of perspective, to become a tool for spatial relation, a signifier for another level of "figuration". Line becomes a tool for articulating space in all of its variations.

It is precisely this aspect of Lipchitz's work that has always been appreciated in books on 20th century sculpture, although far fewer books have been written on the subject than about painting. Since the publication in 1957 of Robert Goldwater's global overview of 20th century sculpture "*What is modern sculpture?",* there have been few attempts at a similar look at sculpture of the century. Abraham M. Hammacher attempted it with *The Evolution of Modern Sculpture: Tradition and Innovation* (New York, 1969). The first effort that was not in print was an exhibition that took place in the German city of Munster in 1977. It recurs every ten years, as a seasonal exhibition of current diverse trends in the world of sculpture. Toward the end of the seventies two intellectuals offered overviews in the form of essays: Rosalind Krauss wrote *Passages In Modern Sculpture* (New York, 1977) and Harold Osborne wrote *Abstraction and Artifice in Twentieth Century Art* (Oxford, 1979). In 1980, Wenken Park in Riehen, Switzerland was the site for a kind of survey of sculpture from Rodin through Pop Art. In 1984, in Merian Park, Brüglingenm, near Basel, the gallerist Ernst Beyeler displayed 223 pieces produced after 1905, that is, beyond Rodin but also *with* him. That same year saw the publication of *Insights-On Sites: Perspectives on Art In Public Places* (Washington, 1984), edited by Stacy Paleologos Harris. In 1986 the Centre Pompidou in Paris completed the cycle with their exhibition *Qu' est-ce que la sculture moderne?* [What is Modern Sculpture?], curated by Margit Rowell, in some ways a response to Diane Waldman's exhibition of the previous year at the Guggenheim in New York entitled *Transformations in Sculpture* (and the only one that does not include work by Lipchitz). As I said in my essay[17] "Art and Nature and Transformations in Sculpture: New Vision of Territory and Landscape," the value of Lipchitz's sculpture is in his voids, and in his sense of landscape.

Nonetheless, a recent exhibit with over 200 works called "*Negative Space. Trajectories of Sculpture*" at The Center for Art and Media (ZKM) in Karlsruhe incomprehensibly excluded Lipchitz.[18]

The Void in Sculpture, 1932

After *Joie de vivre* (1927), installed in the Cubist garden designed by Mallet-Stevens at Villa Noailles, *Song of the Vowels* (1931) was his second monumental open-air sculpture, created to interact intimately with its natural and architectural surroundings. Its majestic winged form, merging themes of Icarus, birds, and music, is derived from his figures of harp players created in 1928. The piece *The Harpists* makes reference to a harp concert, but Lipchitz deliberately makes the title in plural because the image that comes to him appears to be multiple, and not a simple representation of lived experience. The poet Georges Limbour, a contributor to George Bataille's magazine *Documents* dedicated these verses to him: "It is a wind and sun instrument, it is a monumental gateway for clouds, rain, lightning, thunder and sunlight."[19] Le Corbusier describes Lipchitz's piece at Pradet's house this way: "When we go down the small stairway to the ground, we see a large statue by Lipchitz appear, a stele whose final palmette unfolds in the sky above the mountains."[20]

At the same time as he made this piece, between late 1931 and early 1932, Lipchitz was making countless images of heads resting on a hand, ever more subtle, like *Tête et main*, [Head and Hand], where the face itself disappears or appears, defined only by exterior elements like the hand that the chin rests on; or the face held between two hands that are clasped at the forehead as in *Meditation,* a piece that at the same time transports us to the past, back to 1925. In these *Heads* from 1931-32 there were no more hands, no more meditation, to the contrary: Lipchitz was modeling the exterior, the head as a shell, as a fortress enclosing a void. The head gave way to the void, and Lipchitz revisited both the approach to space of the 1925 *transparents*, and the subject of meditation. The depth of that focus was articulated by just three masses, the head and the two hands, but the intensity lay in or was "constructed" in that empty space. All of these heads and hands are excellent examples of the theme of melancholy, with the hand resting against the cheek. It was the search for the value of life within the depths of the human skull, in the disappearance of the mass of the brain—the head as a cave, as a symbol of an energy that is not expressed—a fortress that encloses a mystery. The head became a pantheon and a refuge, it was architecture, a place for encounter between interior and exterior space.

There is a single example of a plaster piece that had great influence at the time and was shared in Maurice Raynal's book (Paris, 1947). Many have seen it as an inspiration for later compositions by Henry Moore such as *Helmet* (1939), similar in size to *Helmet Head* (1950). The essence of that piece was later echoed in the enormous pieces in the sixties such as *Atom Piece* (Working Model for *Nuclear Energy*), 1964-5, sketch for the large outdoor piece *Nuclear Energy,* commissioned by the University of Chicago.

The second head is more open, less helmet-like, and with more irregular shapes. The mass of the skull is leaning a bit, and it rests on supports that are more chiseled, dynamic, and irregular. It is a head that is shelter but wide open at the same time. There is no clear distinction between the inside and the outside as with previous ones, rather there a sense of continuous flow between the space of the empty head and the space that penetrates it. It is more dynamic than the previous one, more organic in its movement, although both have that sense of mystery that would be of such great interest to the other sculptors of the time. In the autobiography Lipchitz points out: "Some of these studies of head and hands were formal explorations of interior or negative sculptural space, and the interest in this problem led me in 1932 to a series of sketches of helmet or skull heads in which the interior space is open and enveloped by a skin or bone structure pierced with great eye holes."[21]

Head (1932) was another piece that had an enormous influence at the time, not only on Henry Moore but also on Barbara

Jacques Lipchitz with Le Corbusier in Brittany, 1928.

Hepworth. Lipchitz built his poetics with that magic of forms, by capturing feelings that, more than figures, generated rhythms, using as a tool *the interaction of forms,* anticipating Moore's play with empty and full. Lipchitz did not envy the success of Moore's reclining Figures or sculptural voids at all. It was only in his correspondence with his first wife Berthe that he let some bitterness slip out, for example, when in a letter dated November 29 he made the following observation about Henry Moore's 1949 exhibition in Paris: "...as for the helmet, it's nothing more than my empty heads – the content, a sort of paraphrase of *Figure* and my *transparents.*"[22]

Other Significant Works

In addition to the aforementioned works there are three other pieces in the exhibition that deserve special mention: *Portrait* (a portrait of poet Raymond Radiguet, 1920), *Study for Figure* (1927) and *The Cry* (1928-29).

Portrait, depicting poet Raymond Radiguet is an exceptional work of art. Lipchitz was always skilled at portraiture and frequently used his own friends, like Cesar Sophianopulos, as models in the early years in Paris. While he was working on the bust of the young poet Radiguet, he also made portraits of Jean Cocteau (1889-1963) in granite, marble, and bronze, and the following year, Gertrude Stein was his model. Regarding his approach to portraiture, which helped him to earn a living and the distinction of being one of the finest sculptors of the 20th century, Lipchitz said, in his own words: "during 1932 and 1933 I returned to portraiture, of which the most interesting to me was the portrait of Géricault. I have always been a great admirer of this painter, a genius who died young, and I have some paintings of his... I wanted to make the portrait as realistic as possible, so I checked documents and existing portraits of him. This was my homage to a great artist whom I loved very much."[23] During his American period he made portraits of a large number of friends and celebrities including presidents John F. Kennedy and Lyndon B. Johnson.

Study for Figure, (1927), is an enormously important piece. It is the maquette for the large piece located at MoMA called *Figure* that Alfred Barr Jr. bought from him in 1936 on a visit to Boulogne. *Figure* (1926-30) is a powerful totem-like piece that embodies all of the precedents laid out between the ideas of Cubism and primitive art. The sculptor related an amusing anecdote about his encounter with Barr, who was sent to visit him by his New York art dealer Joseph Brummer. "When the show was over, I was taking the plaster back in a truck when a man came up to me and started to speak. Since I was busy, I asked him to wait and then to help me carry the sculpture. This he did, and then he and his wife rode in the truck with me to Boulogne and helped me unload it, following my orders patiently. Then we sat down and had a glass of wine and the man finally introduced himself as Alfred Barr, director of the MoMA. I was naturally embarrassed, but he was very nice and we became good friends."[24]

The influence of this piece, as idol, as *art primitive* for the 20th century, speaks to present generations, as sculptor Nathan Mabry observed: "I've always been drawn to this piece -- a prime example of a modernist looking at ethnographic imagery and translating it into avant-garde sculpture. From what I've read, Lipchitz was looking at Senufo rhythm pounders from the Ivory Coast, fertility symbols pounded against the ground during rituals. When I first saw this piece as a student, it seemed alien and wild to me, and from certain angles completely abstract. But you can also see a standing woman, with an oval head and two eyes on each side. And the more I look, the more sensual and erotic it becomes. For my new gallery show at Cherry and Martin, I sculpted a version of it in clay and cast it in recycled aluminum -- turning it into a fountain that cries from all eyes."[25]

Jacques Lipchitz and Alberto Giacometti, Hyères, April 1931, from the album of Marie-Laure de Noailles.

Study for Figure was inspired by an idea he had for Coco Chanel in 1921, and by the landscape of Ploumanac'h, where he and his wife Berthe first visited in 1923, and again in 1925 and 1926, this time with Le Corbusier and his wife. It was there, on the pink granite coast of Ploumanac'h in the French region of Brittany that Lipchitz realized that his sculptures had to change from being simple Cubist formal exercises. They needed to become formal "encounters" on a large scale; his sculpture had to be in public spaces. In a letter written in August 1923 to Alfred Barnes, who was building his foundation in Merion, Pennsylvania, Lipchitz wrote: "This summer in Ploumanac'h, a country of strange rocks, I reflected a great deal while contemplating these rocks with their curious balance. And as a result, I'm thinking of applying it to the open-air statues. Garden statues mainly, on which I plan to focus most of my work. It is an exciting issue to which modern sculpture must make a fresh contribution."[26]

It was on this coast that Lipchitz began to contemplate monumentality, the need to abandon the constraints of sculpture in the form of maquettes to create large-scale works in the open air. He craved the physicality of working on a grand scale. The ideas of mass and equilibrium, of balance and the void, reappear in these pieces, as if engaging his earlier reliefs and mounted works in an unstable game. It was here that Lipchitz composed a *Figure* in three parts: two overlapping pedestals and a relief like the bathers. Lipchitz revisited his ideas for the Chanel garden along with Brancusi's idea of incorporating the pedestal into the sculpture.

He was in awe of the massive rocks, and of their size relative to the bathers on the beach. He set to work on a series of pieces that reflected two elements in equilibrium: on the top, a woman in bas-relief reclining on suggested ocean waves. He described these rocks as these objects "held in a delicate equilibrium" in his book *Life in Sculpture* (New York, 1972). In Ploumanac'h, the shapes of the rocks facing the sea, one immense boulder piled on the other, eroded by the water and the wind, gave the impression of an inconceivable equilibrium, both precarious and fixed. Picasso had spent summers with Olga Kokhlova (1891-1955) on this same coast, at Dinard's villa in 1922 and again in 1928. Dinard is close to St. Malo, and not far from the bay of Mont-Saint-Michel. His sketchbooks from this period reflect the mesmerizing attraction of those rocks, and their special way of fitting together.

The impact of landscape on abstract sculpture in the 20th century took three directions: from monument to landscape as in Brancusi, from the human body to landscape as in Bourdelle and Maillol (and later William Tucker or Magdalena Abakanowicz), or from landscape to sculpture, as in Lipchitz and Picasso, and later Barbara Hepworth.

Dinard, Ploumanac'h, the granite rocks near Trébeurden in northern Brittany, Locmariaquer, not far from the collection of megalithic sites at Carnac: all of those were the old haunts that lingered in the visual memories of the artists. In the thirties, those artists began to reexamine concepts of the avant-garde while, at the same time beginning to synthesize those very ruptures with tradition. Once beyond the frenzied pull of the "modern movements" like Cubism, the variations on constructivism, and the formalist experiences of Kandinsky and the Bauhaus, post-Cubist synthesis would make use of all of the formal breakthroughs and blend them with the more literary or fantastical experiences of the surrealists, or look back in time at earlier landscapes sculpted prior to the Bronze age. Most importantly, they had a newfound awareness of landscape, and of the megaliths both in England and French Brittany in particular.

The third piece is *The Cry* (1928-29), closely related to *The couple* (1929) and *Encounter* (1929). I will not recount the well-known history of this piece here, except to say it was poorly received when first exhibited due to its sexual connotations which would not raise any eyebrows today. But I will say that one of Lipchitz's defenders, Christian Zervos, did not like the piece, and so stated in his essay "*Notes sur la sculpture contemporaine. À propos de la récente Exposition Internationale de Sculpture en la Galerie Georges Bernheim, Paris*" [Notes on Contemporary Sculpture. On the Recent International Sculpture Exhibition at Galerie

Georges Bernheim, Paris] in the magazine *Cahiers d'Art*.[27]

While he praised Picasso and the diachronic values of primitive art, Zervos was shifting his gaze toward the new generation of artists, highlighting three sculptors: Henri Laurens, Jacques Lipchitz, and Alberto Giacometti. Even so, he disapproved of Lipchitz's *Couple* which he called *L'Amour* [Love]—because it embodied "the mistake of lingering over an action." Lipchitz's blunt response is interesting:

"I'll take advantage of this opportunity to say a few words about your notes on contemporary sculpture published in the last edition of Cahiers d'Art, notes that I read with very great interest. This does not mean that I am in complete agreement with you. Starting with what you say about the relationship between sculptors and the spirit of the Renaissance. It always seemed to me that the sculptor Donatello was one of the first sculptors to embody this spirit. And if other sculptors continued to be inspired by the Gothic spirit during the height of the Renaissance, there were also painters who were rebels in their time. The same way, in our time, the sculptor Rodin, more than any school and more than any painter of his time, gave us the spirit of freedom with the spectacle of nature...he has contributed more than anyone else to defining the spirit of our time. "Meanwhile, Cubism arrived. All painters were affected to one extent or another," you said. And I say to myself that some ambitious painters were affected. You continue, "only sculptors remained outside this movement," and I say to myself, some sculptors have been affected by the movement. Archipenko, Brancusi [sic] and since 1913, me especially. But I am not one to correct mistakes. I am not drawn to doing that. I am more interested in talking about your comment on my Couple. Why do you call it Love?[28] (Draft of the letter from Jacques Lipchitz to Christian Zervos, February 9, 1930. Museum of Art and Jewish History, Paris)

Lipchitz's Drawings

His drawings, spanning from 1910 until 1932, are also a part of this exhibition. All of the elements that appeared earlier in his sculptures are visible in them, from his early very realist influences to the first attempts at Cubism, as seen in the two excellent drawings *Woman with Fan* (1913) and *Spanish Woman with Fan* (1914), (probably made during his stay with Diego Rivera in Spain), to *Woman in Profile* (1910), so closely aligned with Modigliani, and the heads of 1930-32, so reminiscent of Henry Moore's works yet to come. Lipchitz, like other great sculptors of the 20th century such as Alexander Calder, Henry Moore himself, or Eduardo Chillida, made working on paper a part of his practice, always as a tool for his visual explorations. He drew both before and after working on his sculptural pieces, no doubt due to the power of drawing as a starting point for sculpture, and its usefulness as a tool to explore different themes and shapes that would later be translated into three dimensional constructions. We can see Lipchitz's artistic evolution through his drawings, which allow us to witness his experience and his struggle to integrate the idea born both *with* and *from* form.

After an early phase we could call Doric, with his very linear drawings after the style of Modigliani, he began to make drawings that convey a sense of graphic violence characterized by curving lines. Rather than being arranged, form bursts forth out of their *organic chaos*, and the image appears or happens. Lipchitz sets the seriousness of the Cubist vanguard aside to become a new sculptor in the imagery and style of *Laocoonte*. For him, Cubism was a gateway not so much to a style as to a philosophy of looking at space in order to then shape it in his own way. It was not the idea of movement that interested Lipchitz, however, but the image born of *the interaction of forms*, a notion that had its origins in how Cubism evolved in the hands of the Italian Futurists, especially by Umberto Boccioni with his sculpture *Development of a Bottle in Space* (1912, now at MoMA, donated by the family of the sculptor Maillol). Lipchitz was influenced, like all great artists, by the history of art. Three influences in particular stand out: the vertical religiosity and forms of El Greco, the denial of geometry in search of the rhythm of the mark that he learned from Tintoretto and Goya, and the spatial tension of Mannerism and Baroque art.

Whether in charcoal or wax colored pencils, we can also see the "sculptural" interest in those drawings by Lipchitz, both in how he studies the possible impact of light in the bronzes (sculpture) that he has in his mind, and in other ways, as with the positioning of the sculpture and of its pedestal, or in how to mount or create a base in a way that unifies the piece as a whole. The various approaches to drawing, whether rapid sketches of ideas, drawings that work out a sculpture ahead of time, or as conduits to a graphic image—a way to realize his etchings, for Lipchitz they are all intimately tied to his way of modeling and achieving a certain kind of figuration that is not immediately apparent, but that is revealed if we linger and look for a moment.

In them and with them we can see that the artist's vocabulary grows out of a figuration that blends biblical themes (both Jewish and Christian readings) with themes from mythology (both Greek and Roman) while blending in a social message. It is a figuration that is continuously revealed by looking, creating formal movement with the bodies. These are a *sculptor's drawings*, drawings by someone who thinks in three dimensions—someone with an immense talent for composition.

From Cubism to the *Inter-Relationship* of Forms

This great artist, forced to emigrate in 1909 from Lithuania to France, and later to the United States in 1941, always brought his ideas and his talent with him. His work speaks not only of exile, but also of hardship (in the mid-1950s his New York studio burned down) and above all of the resilience of the human being, with references to both Greek mythology and the Old Testament. With his personal lexicon of forms, Lipchitz revisits the images of different religious traditions to create a poem, *for him, a visual poem,* that like mystical lyrics, transcends the everyday meaning of words *in search of the ineffable*, to find a *transcendental sculptural experience.*

It would seem that while the Lithuanian sculptor outgrew his early technical beginnings, moving from classical modeling to Cubism, he was also building a special imaginary at the same time, in those seminal years from 1911 to 1925, one that would take his work far beyond myth and biblical stories. He freed himself from academicism upon his arrival in Paris, and he would later leave behind the impasses of Cubism and his appreciation for African sculpture to discover the value of the void (the interaction of forms) in his *Transparents*, which are not so far removed from the serpentine figures of the Mannerists. Lipchitz saw that he could create a language that blended all of the motifs, from the biblical and Greco-Roman, from the Hellenistic and the Christian Baroque; he understood that his hands searched for a formal archetype like Aby Warburg's (1866-1929) *pathosformeln* in the history of art, or Carl Gustav Jung's (1875-1961) archetypes of the collective unconscious.

Lipchitz, once established in New York, developed a very personal language of *interaction of forms* that would become his immediately recognizable style; a language that went beyond the literal sense of characters from Scripture or mythology to *re-create* them in his singular sculptures. It is a figuration that is not immediate, but which is gradually revealed in the round, a figuration that is not as abrupt as it looks at first glance, a figuration that is discovered in the looking, with its sense of formal movement created by the figures. The feeling of movement that comes from the *inter-penetration* of form and volume, the interplay of light and dense line, the kind of narrative (be it schematic or on a monumental scale)—those works speak to us now, through their difficult but compelling forms, of the power of human action and the struggle for a better world. But this sculpture as inter-penetration of forms was made many years ago, in those years in Paris.

Jacques Lipchitz and Pablo Picasso in Antibes, France, 1954.

— Kosme de Barañano

Kosme de Barañano is full tenure Professor of Art History at the University Miguel Hernandez in Elche (since 2004), and full tenure Professor of Art History at the University of the Basque Country (1989-2000). He was an Invited Professor at the Kunsthistorisches Institut at the University of Heidelberg, Germany (1983-1989). He worked at the following museums: Hirschhorn Museum and Sculpture Garden, Washington, D.C. (1986); Museo Nacional Reina Sofia as Deputy Director (1989-1990); and the IVAM, Valencia as Executive Director (2000-2004). He has curated more than 70 exhibitions (and edited their corresponding catalogues) in different museums in Europe and in the United States and Japan, for example, Alberto Giacometti, Eduardo Chillida, Philip Guston, and Max Beckmann.

NOTES

1.Hilton Kramer, "Why Jacques Lipchitz Was Left by Wayside: Aspired to Greatness", in *The Observer* 03/15/2004.
2.Waldemar George, "Jacques Lipchitz" in the magazine *L'Amour de l'Art*, August 1921, p. 257.
3.The magazine *L'Architecture vivante* was an avant-garde magazine edited by Jean Badovici and published in Paris by Albert Morancé. Twenty-one issues appeared between 1923 and 1933. *L'Architecture vivante*, New York: Da Capo Press, 1975.
4.Paul Dermée, "Lipchitz" *L'Esprit Nouveau,* Paris, number 2, 1920, p. 170, a magazine that he himself ran.
5.In *Jacques Lipchitz Quotes*. (online) available from: http://www.inspirationalstories.com/quotes/copy-nature-and-you-infringe-on-the-of-jacques-lipchitz-quote/). This citation is used in the "Brown University admissions application" along with this question: "With this in mind, describe a moment when your perspective changed."
6.Archive of Musée d'Art et Histoire du Judaïsme, Paris, cited by Anabela de Araujo, op. cit. 76.
7.Letter from Charles de Noailles to Lipchitz from Paris on June 5, 1926, private archives, in the book by Alexandre Mare, Stephane Boudin-Lestienne, *Charles et Marie-Laure de Noailles. Mécènes du XX siecle*, Bernard Chauveau Edition, Hyeres Paris 2018, p.126 note.
8.Letter from Lipchitz to Berthe, February 25, 1928, Mnam Paris.
9.Letter from Jacques Lipchitz to Charles de Noailles, October 1, 1927, in the book by Alexandre Mare, Stephane Boudin-Lestienne, *Charles et Marie-Laure de Noailles. Mécènes du XX siecle*, Bernard Chauveau Edition, Hyeres Paris 2018, p.127.
10.In the first international conference *Support Surface: The support as a field for research. The River*, Fundación Cañada Blanch, Valencia, 2010.
11. Jacques Lipchitz, *My Life in Sculpture by Jacques Lipchitz with H.H. Arnason,* in The Documents of 20th Century Art, edited by Robert Motherwell, Viking Press, New York 1972, p.85
12.op. cit. p.86.
13.op. cit. p. 81.
14.14 is Juan Gris's answer to a survey in the *Bulletin de la vie artistique,* January 1, 1925. Gris had given a talk at the Sorbonne on May 15, 1924, translated into English as "On the Possibilities of Painting" in *Transatlantic Review* number 6 from June-July of 1924.
15.Christopher Green, Picasso: Architecture and Vertigo, Yale University Press 2005 p. 180.
16.Alan G. Wilkinson, from Grove Art Online, © 2009 Oxford University Press.
17.Kosme de Barañano "Arte y naturaleza en las transformaciones de la escultura: nueva vision del territorio y del paisaje" [Art and Nature and Transformations in Sculpture: New Vision of Territory and Landscape] at the first international *Support Surface* conference: *The support as a field for research. The River*, Fundación Cañada Blanch, Valencia, 2010.
18."*Negative Space. Trajectories of Sculpture*" at the Center for Art and Media (ZKM) in Karlsruhe (06.04.2019 – 11.08.2019, curators: Peter Weibel, and Anett Holzheid, Daria Mille). According to the curators: "The trajectories of spatial sculpture will be traced along the lines of cubism, constructivism, neo-constructivism, minimal art to present-day installative immersive environments. Jacques Lipchitz does not appear at all, not even after Eduardo Chillida. Later they contextualized the exhibition: The exhibition "Negative Space" endeavors to change the dominating view of modern and contemporary sculpture by telling a different story. "With the aim to investigate the relationship between sculpture and space in a decidedly spatial way, the presented art works address the sculptural phenomenon in relation to diverse spatial concepts: Open spaces, surrounding, hollow and intermediate spaces, mirror, light and shadow spaces, virtual data spaces, etc. The exhibition offers a comprehensive overview of the art of sculpture, which – in contrast to the traditional concept – is committed to contour, emptiness, and levitation." The exhibit "Negative Space" was aimed at changing the dominant vision of modern and contemporary sculpture, telling a different story. "With the goal of investigating the relationship between sculpture and space in a way that is decidedly spatial, the works of art displayed address the phenomenon of sculpture in relation to various spatial concepts: open spaces, adjacent, hollow, or in-between spaces, mirrors, spaces of light and shadow, spaces of virtual data, etc." The exhibit offers a global vision of the artform of sculpture, which, in contrast with traditional concepts, is involved with contour, the void, and levitation."
19.Georges Limbour, *Spectateur des arts, Écrits sur la peinture* 1924-1969, Le Bruit du temps, 2013 (edition prepared by Martine Colin-Picon and F. Nicol). Also in *Soleils bas. Suivi de Poèmes, contes et récits* (1919-1968), Preface by Michel Leiris, Gallimard "Poésie" Collection (No. 82), Gallimard Paris 1972.
20.On the relationship between Helene de Mandrot-Le Corbusier, see: A. Baudin "*Le Corbusier et Hélène de Mandrot, une relation problématique*" in *Le Corbusier, la Suisse et les Suisses*, Editions de La Villette, Paris, 2006, pp. 148-165. For the citation about Lipchitz's work: Le Corbusier, *Œuvre complète*, vol.1: 1929-1934, Zurich, Artemis, 1966, pp. 61-62.
21.Op.cit. p. 127.
22.Letter to Berthe 29.11.1949, Mnam Paris.
23.Op.cit. p. 127.
24.Op.cit. p.135.
25.As told to Jori Finkel, in " It speaks to me: Nathan Mabry on Jacques Lipchitz's 'Figure' at the Norton Simon Museum", in *Los Angeles Times,* January 11, 2011.
26.In *Correspondance de Jacques Lipchitz adressée à Berthe Kitrosser (1948-1972)* very accurately annotated by Anne-Marie Zucchelli and Brigitte Léal in the Centre Pompidou París, Musée Nancy, 2004 catalog.
27.*Cahiers d'Art*, no. 10, 1929 pp. 465-472.
28.Draft of Jacques Lipchitz's letter to Christian Zervos, February 9, 1930. Museum of Jewish Art and History, Paris.

Woman and Gazelles, 1911, bronze, edition of 7, 30 x 46 x 8 1/8 in., 76.2 x 116.8 x 20.6 cm

Pregnant Woman, 1912, bronze, edition of 7, 24 1/4 x 4 3/4 x 5 1/2 in., 61.6 x 12.1 x 14 cm

Woman in Profile, ca.1910-12, pencil on paper, 16 1/8 x 10 1/4 in., 41 x 26 cm

Left: *Young Girl Sitting,* 1912, pencil on paper, 8 x 5 in., 20.3 x 12.7 cm
Right: *Woman with Fan,* 1913, pencil on paper, 13 3/8 x 10 1/4 in., 34 x 26 cm

Spanish Woman with Fan, 1914, pencil and colored crayon on paper, 8 x 6 1/4 in., 20.3 x 15.9 cm

Sculpture, 1915, bronze, edition of 7, 36 7/8 x 9 x 7 1/4 in., 93.7 x 22.9 x 18.4 cm

Seated Figure, 1915, bronze, edition of 7, 34 1/4 x 8 1/2 x 6 1/4 in., 87 x 21.6 x 15.9 cm

Mother and Child (Study for a Standing Woman), 1915, crayon and pencil on paper, 15 x 10 1/4 in., 38.1 x 26 cm

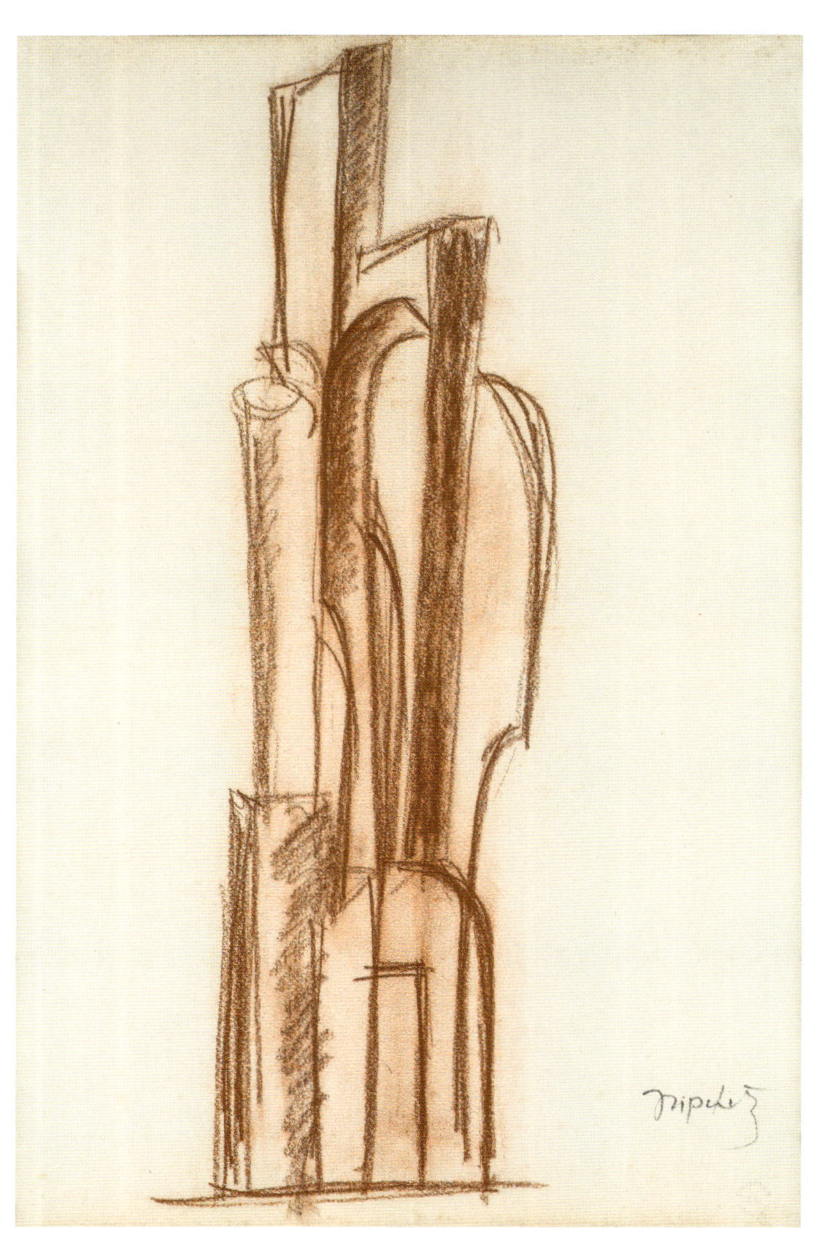

Study for a Statue (Cubist Study), 1915, sanguine on paper, 18 7/8 x 12 3/8 in., 47.9 x 31.4 cm

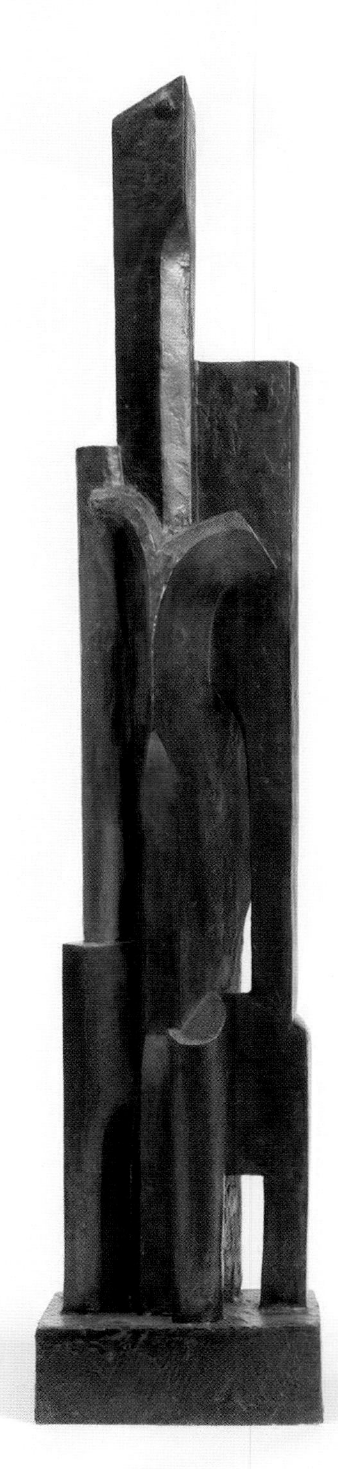

Standing Figure, 1916, bronze, edition of 7, 41 1/4 x 8 1/2 x 6 1/2 in., 104.8 x 21.6 x 16.5 cm

Sculpture, 1916, bronze, edition of 7, 45 1/2 x 13 1/4 x 14 1/4 in., 115.6 x 33.7 x 36.2 cm

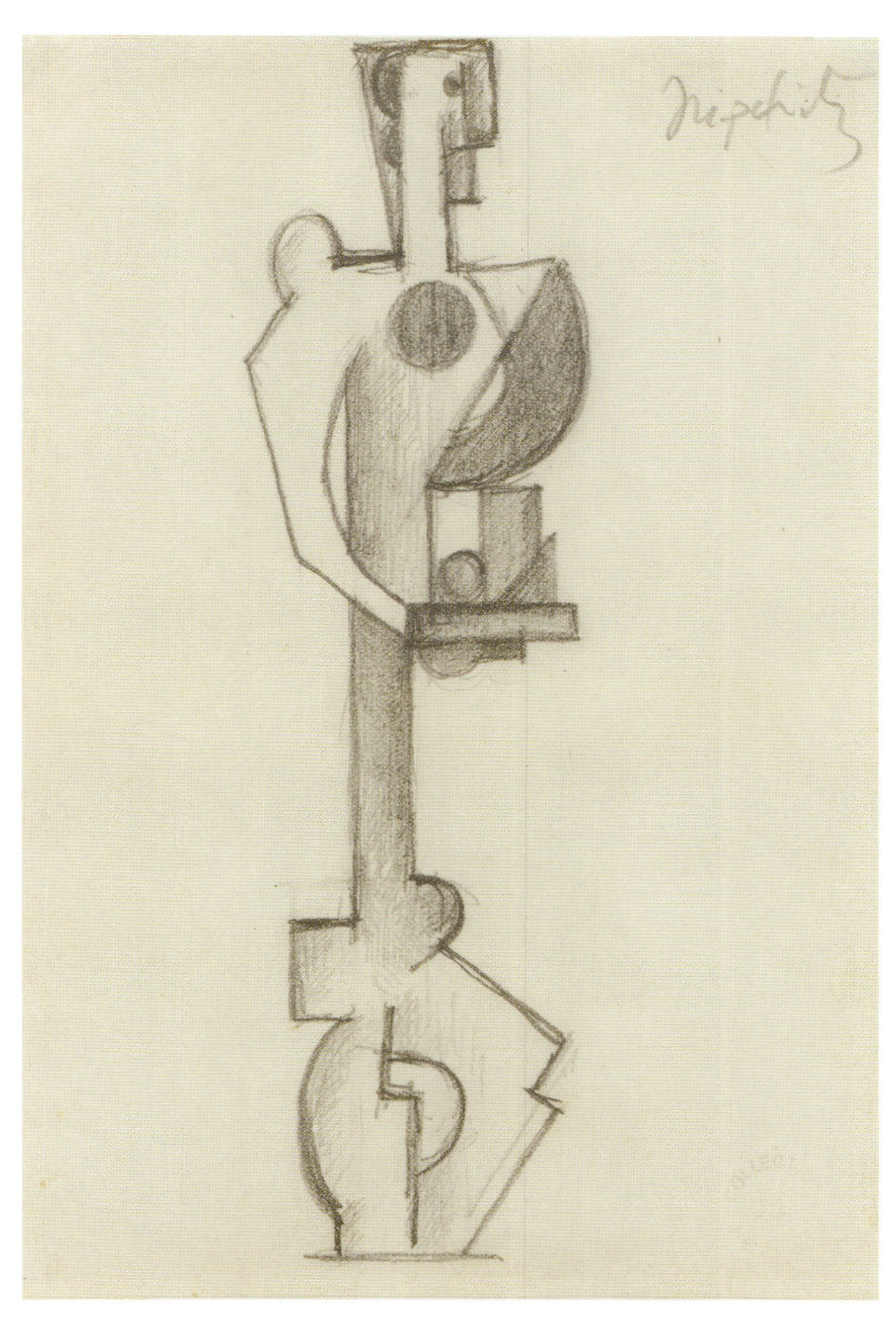

La serveuse, 1915, pencil on paper, 6 3/4 x 4 7/8 in., 17.2 x 12.4 cm

Baigneuse (Bather), 1917, bronze, edition of 7, 34 7/8 x 13 1/4 x 12 3/4 in., 88.6 x 33.7 x 32.4 cm

Bather III, 1917, bronze, edition of 7, 28 1/4 x 10 x 10 in., 71.8 x 25.4 x 25.4 cm

Bas Relief, 1918, stone, unique, 23 x 13 x 3 1/2 in., 58.4 x 33 x 8.9 cm

Still Life, 1918, bronze, edition of 7, 27 1/8 x 21 3/4 x 3 5/8 in., 68.9 x 55.3x 9.2 cm

Still Life, 1919, bronze, edition of 7, 13 1/2 x 17 1/4 x 1 1/8 in., 34.3 x 43.8 x 2.9 cm

Top: *Study for a Relief* (also called *Sheet Music),* 1918, charcoal on paper, 11 7/8 x 10 1/2 in., 30.3 x 26.7 cm
Bottom: *Study for a Bas Relief (Cubist Study),* 1921, pencil on paper, 3 7/8 x 5 1/2 in., 9.8 x 14 cm

Bas Relief II, 1921, polychromed stone, 23 3/4 x 23 3/4 x 3 3/4 in., 60.3 x 60.3 x 9.5 cm

Repentant Magdalene, 1921, bronze, edition of 7, 5 7/8 x 6 x 3 1/4 in., 14.9 x 15.2 x 8.3 cm

Raymond Radiguet, 1922. Photo by Man Ray.

As the decade came to a close, Lipchitz returned to a more realistic, if stylized, mode of portraiture with his busts of artistic friends in Paris, including Coco Chanel, Jean Cocteau, and Gertrude Stein. His sculpture depicting the writer Raymond Radiguet, who died tragically young of typhoid fever at age 20, is one of the most important works from this period. In his own description of this work, Lipchitz writes:

> One of the first [portrait commissions] is the portrait of Raymond Radiguet, 1920. Radiguet was a young poet at that time, no more than 20 years old, a talented man and extraordinarily mature for his age. I think it was Jean Cocteau who introduced him to me and suggested that I do a portrait of him. The young man had an extremely beautiful skull structure, very crisp and clear-cut features, all of which I accentuated. In order to do so, I subordinated the mass of the hair in the plaster and even eliminated it in the bronze. This may be termed more realistic than the earlier portraits done before the war if its precision and in the fact that I sketched in the pupils of the eyes. To me, however, it is still an extremely classical work, one that has some of the qualities of idealism and repose that you find in ancient Greek sculpture.
>
> — from *My Life in Sculpture* by Jacques Lipchitz with H. H. Aranson

Portrait of Raymond Radiguet, 1920, bronze, edition of 7, 12 x 9 1/2 x 8 1/4 in., 30.5 x 24.1 x 21 cm

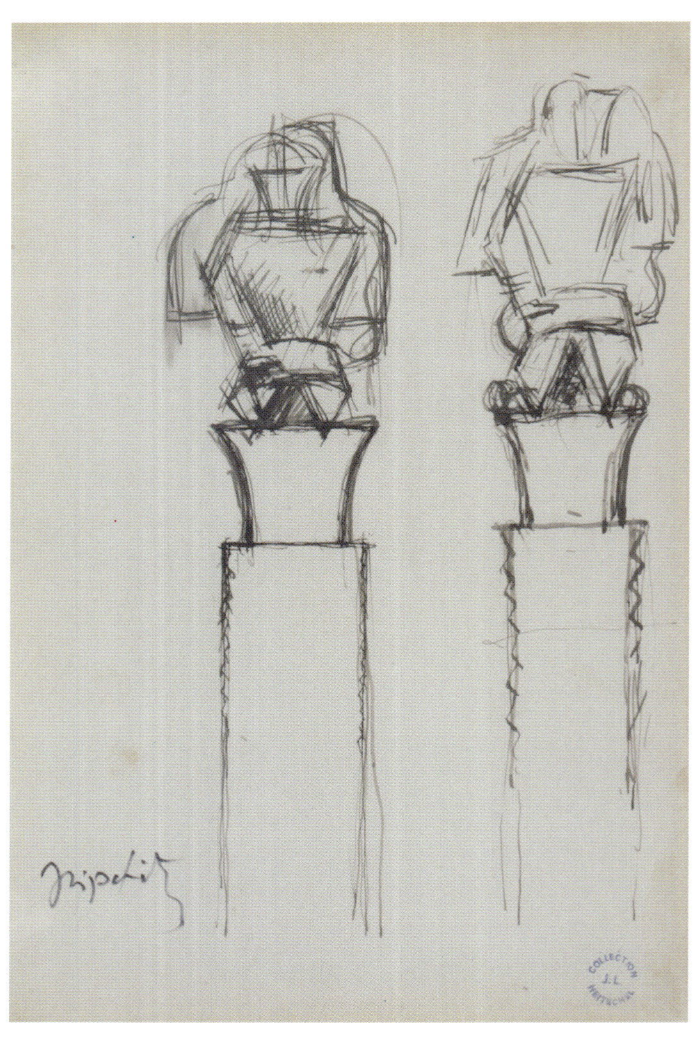

Left: *Study for Sculptures on a Column,* 1920, pen and ink on paper, 11 x 7 7/8 in., 27.9 x 20 cm
Right: *Study for Garden Statue,* 1921, bronze, edition of 7, 5 1/2 x 1 3/4 x 1 3/4 in., 13.7 x 4.5 x 4.5 cm

Study for Figure: Maquette No. 1 ,1927, bronze, edition of 7, 9 x 3 1/4 x 3 in., 24.8 x 8.3 x 7.6 cm

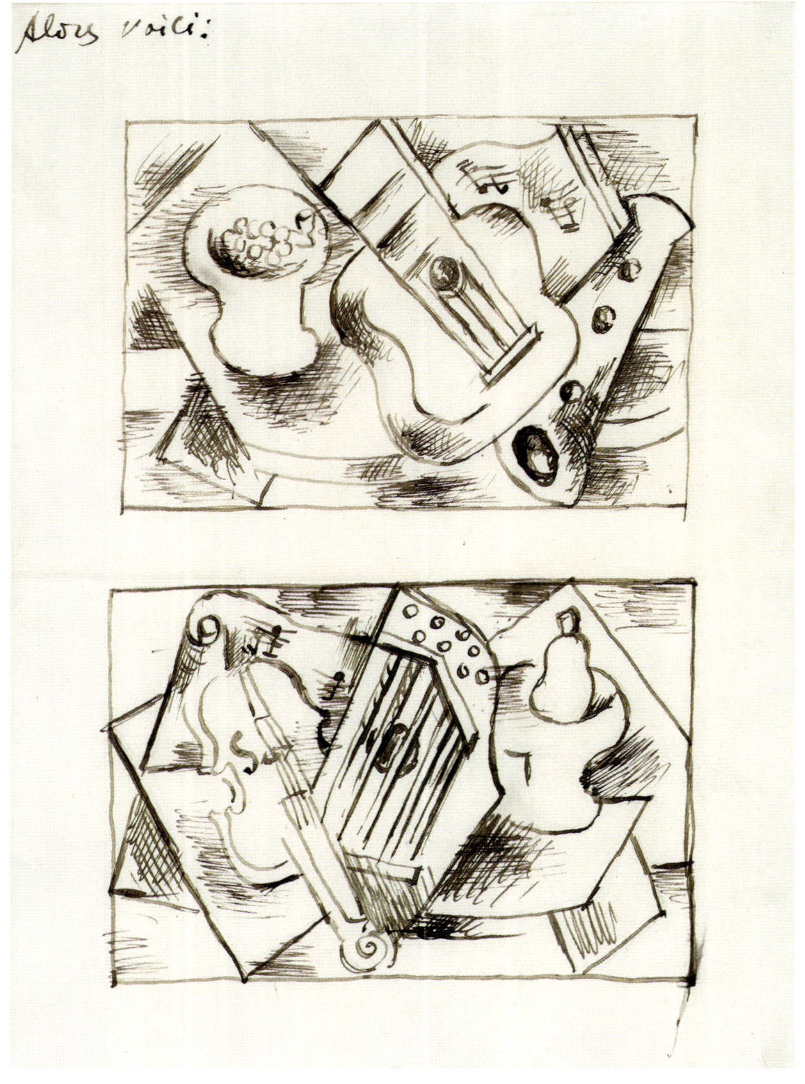

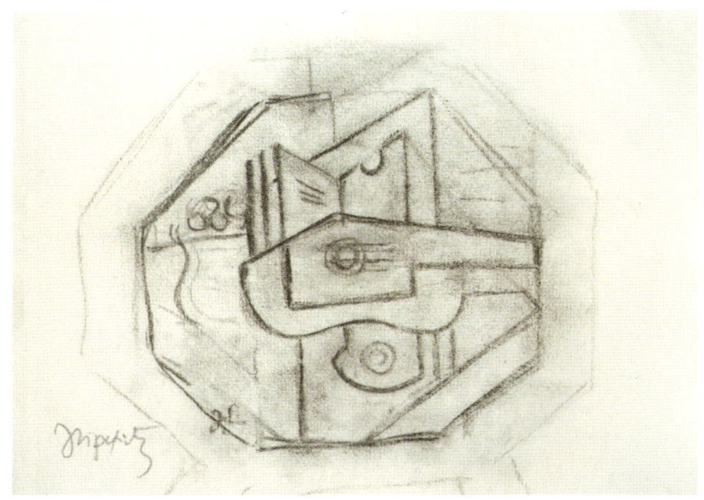

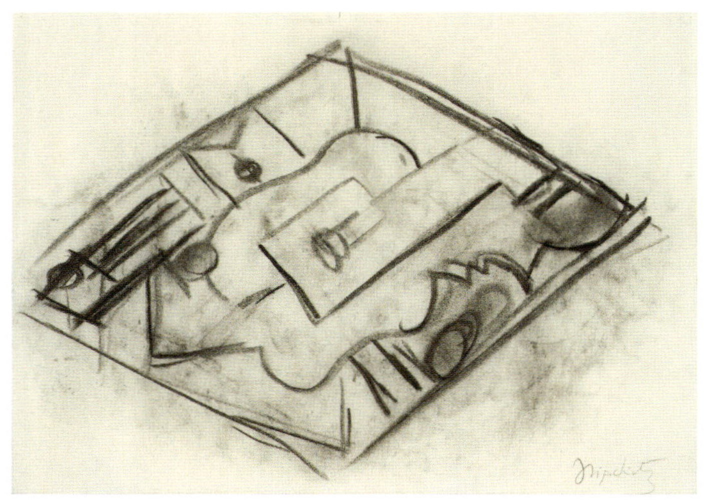

Left: *Still Life with Musical Instruments,* 1923, pen and black ink on paper, 10 1/2 x 8 1/8 in., 26.7 x 20.6 cm
Top Right: *Study for a Bas Relief (Study for a Standing Bas Relief, 1923),* 1922, charcoal on paper, 7 1/8 x 9 1/2 in., 18.1 x 24.1 cm
Bottom Right: *Study for a Bas Relief (Study for Musical Instruments),* ca. 1923, charcoal on paper, 9 7/8 x 14 1/8 in., 25.1 x 35.9 cm

Musical Instruments with Bunches of Grapes, 1922, bronze, edition of 7, 32 1/4 x 42 1/4 x 6 in., 81.9 x 107.3 x 15.2 cm

Musical Instruments with Basket of Fruit and Grapes, 1922, bronze, edition of 7, 31 5/8 x 42 1/8 x 6 1/2 in., 80.3 x 107 x 16.5 cm

Left: *Study for Musical Instruments: Maquette No. 2,* 1923, bronze, edition of 7, 8 x 6 7/8 x 2 3/4 in., 20.3 x 17.5 x 7 cm
Right: *Figure with Guitar: Maquette No. 1*, 1923, bronze, edition of 7, 6 1/4 x 6 3/4 x 2 3/8 in., 15.9 x 17.1 x 6 cm

Musical Instruments, 1923, stone, unique, 19 x 35 x 6 in., 48.3 x 88.9 x 15.2 cm

Harlequin with Mandolin in Oval, 1923, bronze, edition of 7, 49 1/2 x 41 3/4 x 8 in., 125.7 x 106.1 x 20.3 cm

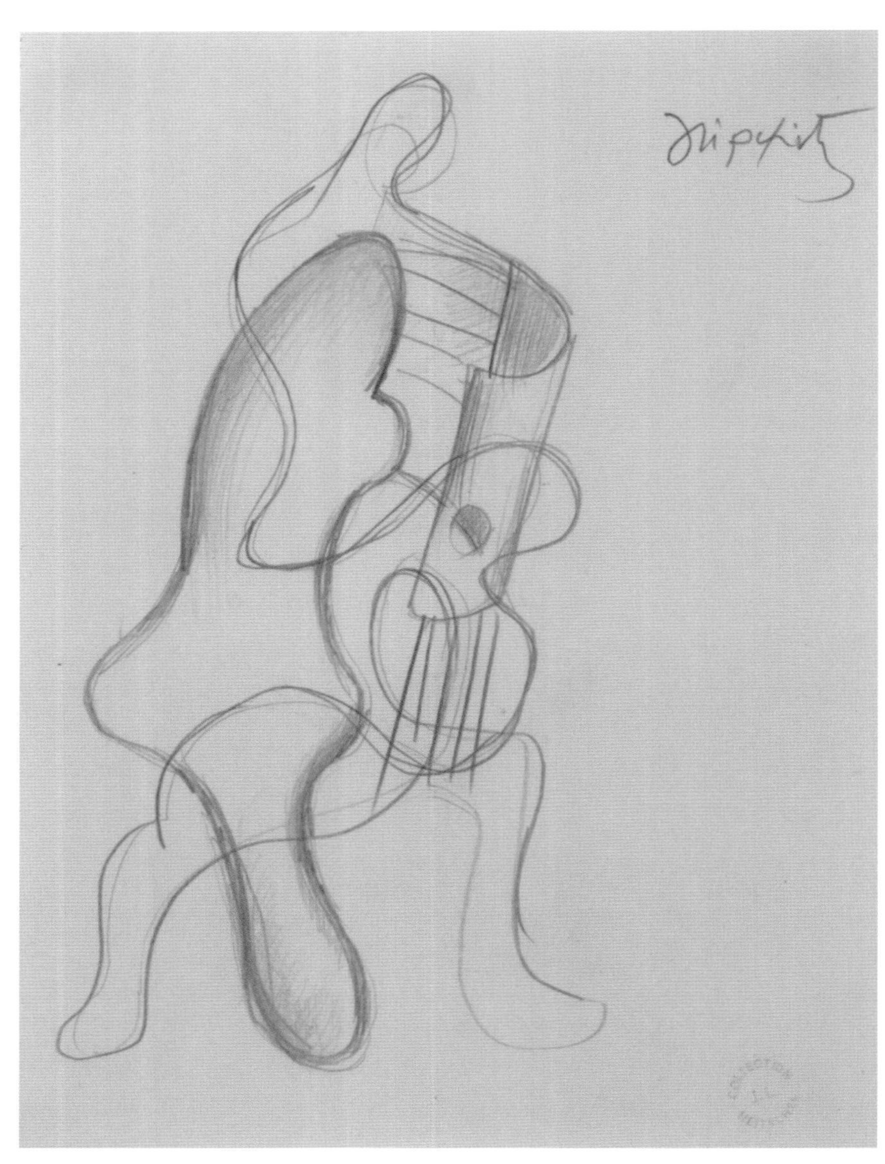

Woman and Guitar (Study for a Sculpture), 1926, pencil on paper, 9 1/8 x 7 in., 23.2 x 17.8 cm

Pierrot, 1925, bronze, unique, 7 3/4 x 4 1/2 x 2 1/2 in., 19.7 x 11.4 x 6.3 cm

Man Leaning on Elbows, 1925, bronze, edition of 7, 4 1/2 x 3 3/8 x 4 in., 11.4 x 8.6 x 10.2 cm

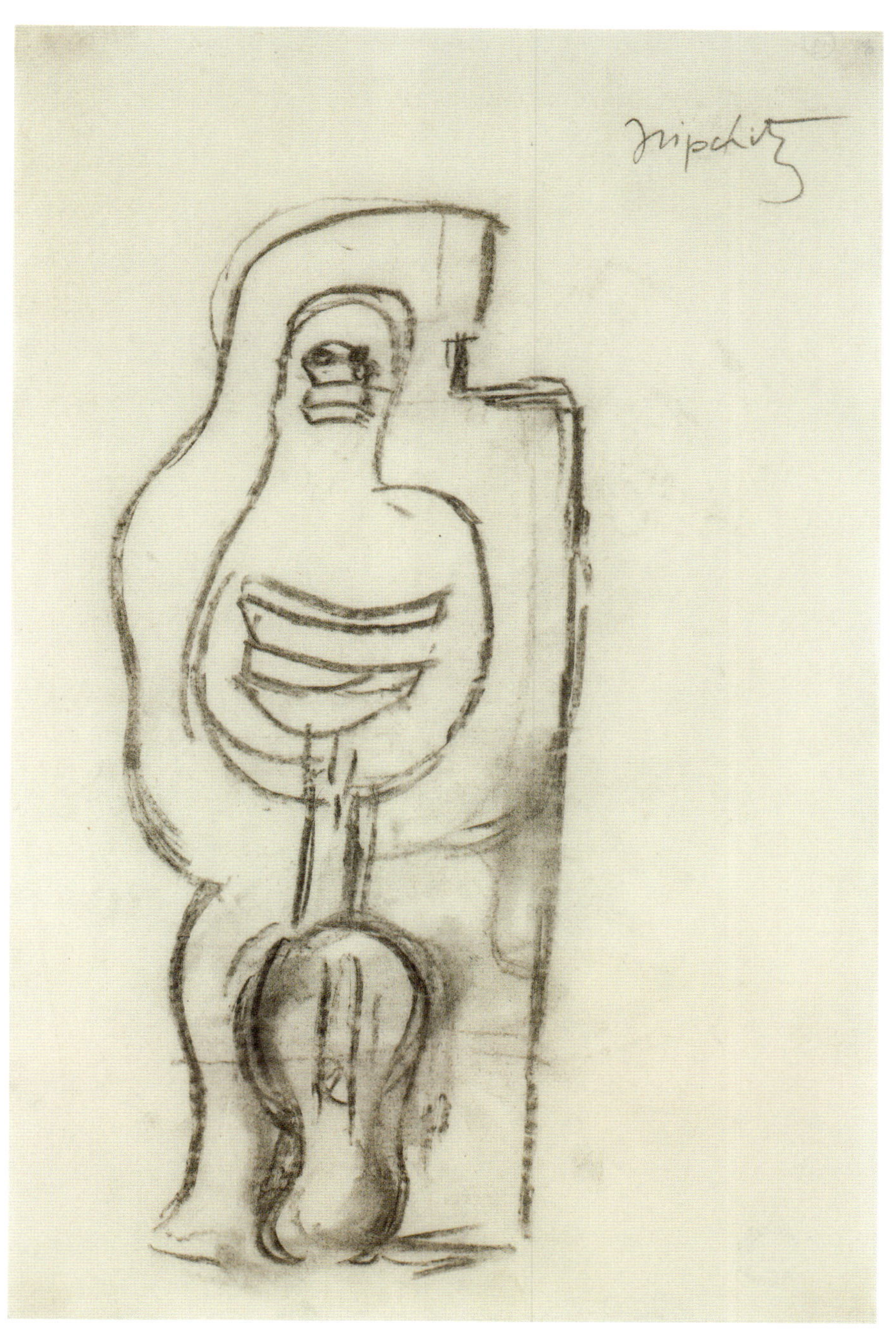

Man and Guitar (Musicians), 1926, charcoal on paper, 12 1/4 x 8 1/4 in., 31.1 x 21 cm

Study for a Transparency (Harlequin 1926), 1926, charcoal on paper, 10 1/4 x 8 1/4 in., 26 x 21 cm

Harlequin with Accordion, 1926, bronze, unique, 9 1/2 x 6 x 7 in., 24.1 x 15.2 x 17.8 cm

Seated Harlequin with Mandolin, 1926, bronze, unique, 8 1/2 x 6 3/4 x 5 in., 21.6 x 17.1 x 12.7 cm

Mardi Gras, 1926, gilded bronze with gold patina, unique, 11 x 6 x 5 3/4 in., 27.9 x 15.2 x 14.6 cm

Woman with Guitar: Maquette No. 2, 1925 bronze, edition of 7, 5 1/8 x 5 1/4 x 3 1/8 in., 13 x 13.3 x 7.9 cm

Musicians, 1928, india ink on paper, 6 1/8 x 9 1/2 in., 15.6 x 24.1 cm

The Cry, 1928-29, bronze, edition of 7, 36 5/8 x 63 3/8 x 37 3/8 in., 93 x 161 x 94.9 cm

The Harpists, 1930, bronze, edition of 7, 21 1/4 x 21 x 10 3/4 in., 54 x 53.3 x 27.3 cm

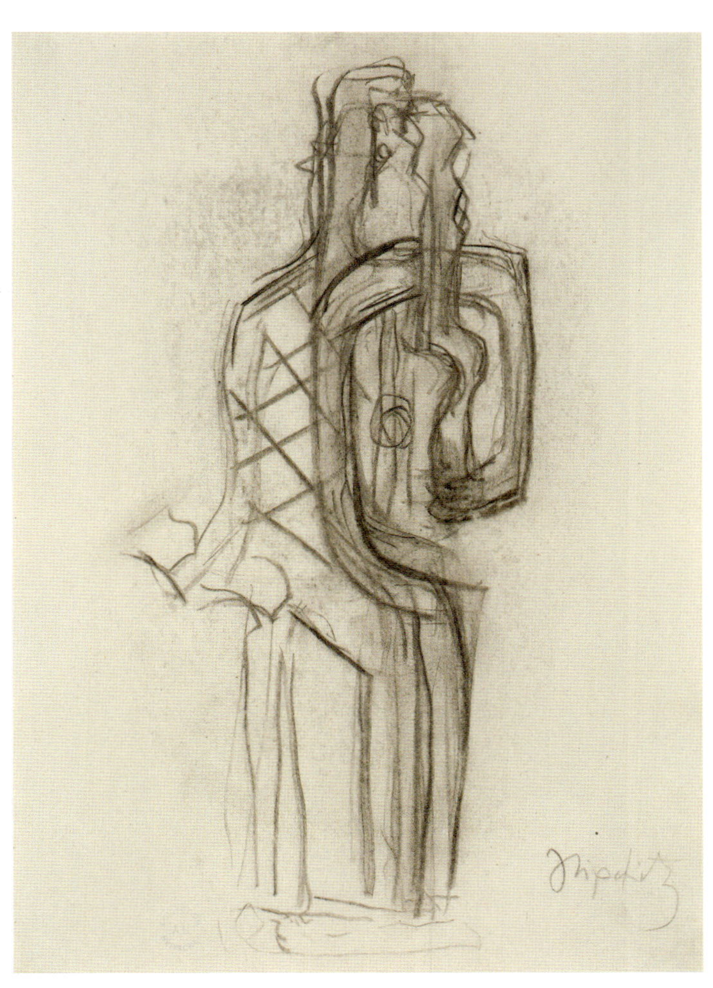

Study for a Transparency (Musician), 1926, charcoal on paper, 12 1/4 x 8 7/8 in., 31.1 x 22.5 cm

Reclining Woman on a Puff, 1929, bronze, edition of 7, 7 1/2 x 8 1/2 x 4 1/4 in., 19.1 x 21.6 x 10.8 cm

The Couple, 1929, bronze, edition of 7, 5 x 7 1/2 x 3 3/4 in., 12.7 x 19.1 x 9.5 cm

Reclining Figure, 1929, bronze, edition of 7, 6 1/4 x 9 x 4 1/4 in., 15.9 x 22.9 x 10.8 cm

Left: *Encounter,* 1929, bronze, edition of 7, 9 3/4 x 4 1/4 x 3 1/2 in., 24.8 x 10.8 x 8.9 cm
Right: *Woman Leaning on a Column (Couple),* 1929, pencil on paper, 8 x 5 in., 20.3 x 12.7 cm

Standing Figure, 1929, bronze, edition of 7, 8 3/8 x 3 5/8 x 3 1/4 in., 21.3 x 9.1 x 8.3 cm

Transparency, 1930, bronze, unique, 15 3/4 x 8 3/4 x 9 in., 40 x 22 x 22.9 cm

Meditation, 1931, bronze, edition of 7, 8 1/4 x 7 x 6 1/2 in., 21 x 17.8 x 16.5 cm

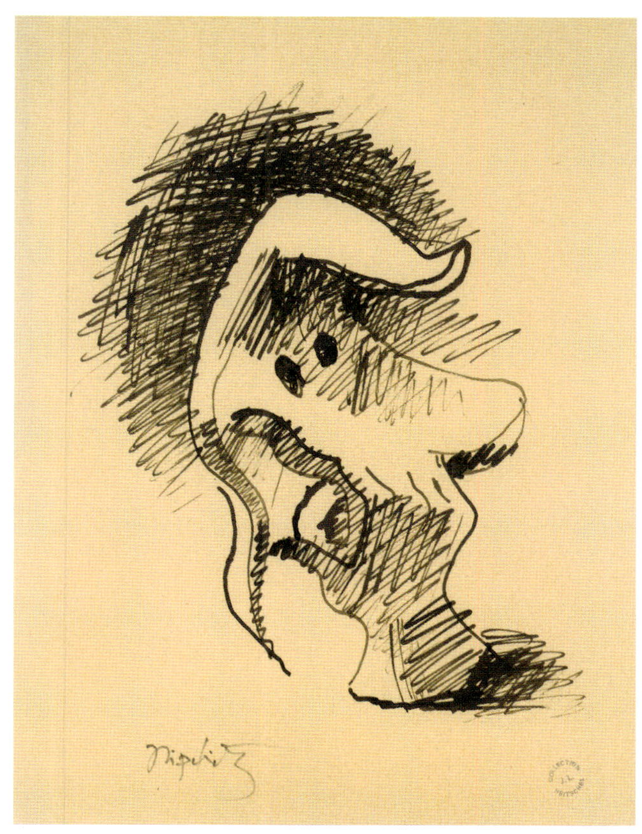

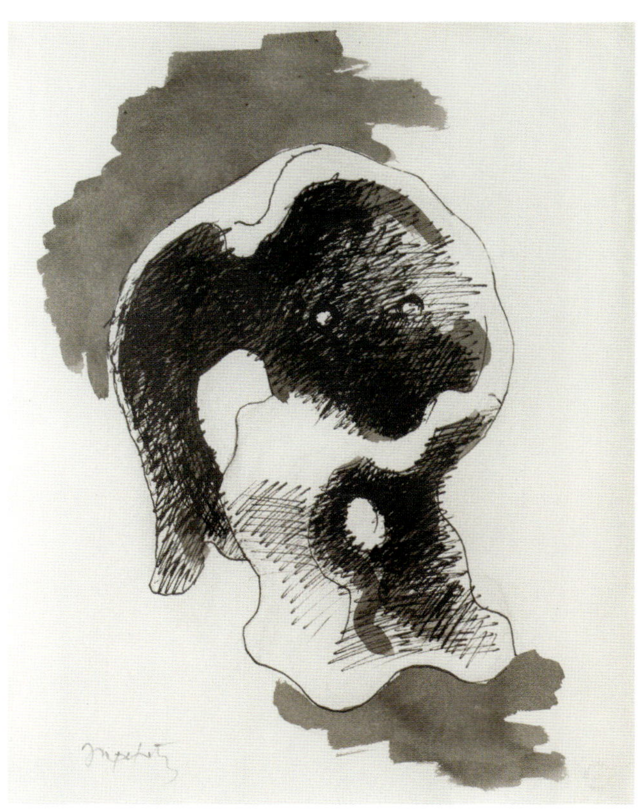

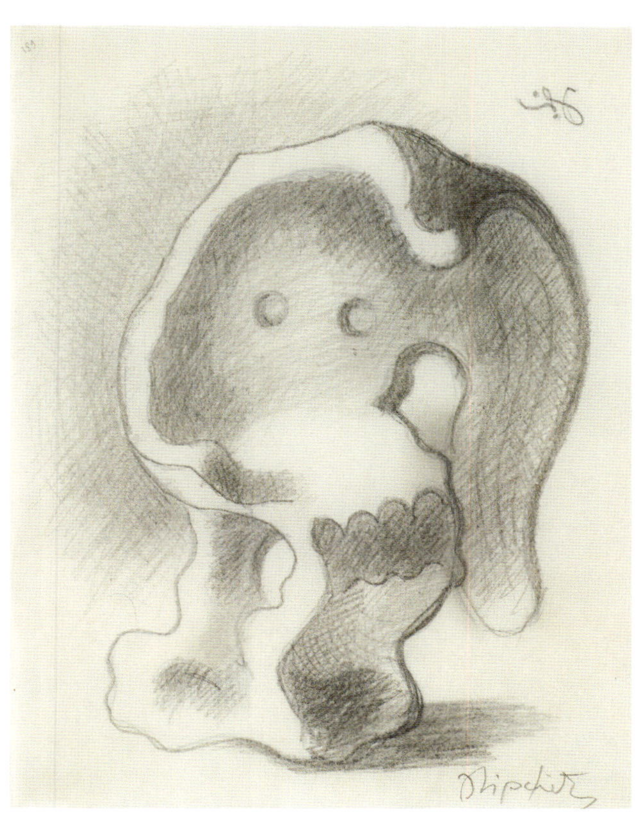

Clockwise from top left:
Hair and Hands (Study for "Head"), 1930, ink on beige paper, 12 5/8 x 9 3/4 in., 32.1 x 24.8 cm
Head & Hands (Studies of head), 1930, ink on paper, 12 5/8 x 9 1/2 in., 32 x 24 cm
Study for "Hands and Hair" (Study for Head), 1932, pencil on paper, 7 7/8 x 6 5/8 in., 20 x 16.8 cm
Study for Head and Hair (Study for Head), 1930, india ink on paper, 16 1/8 x 12 5/8 in., 41 x 32 cm

Head of a Woman and Hair and Hand, 1930, bronze, edition of 7, 6 x 5 1/4 x 3 3/4 in., 15.2 x 13.3 x 9.5 cm

Head, Maquette No. 1, 1932, bronze, edition of 7, 8 1/2 x 5 1/2 x 5 1/2 in., 21.6 x 14 x 14 cm

Jacob and the Angel, 1931, bronze, edition of 7, 36 1/2 x 49 x 25 1/4 in., 92.7 x 124.5 x 64.1 cm

Left: *Study for Jacob and the Angel,* 1931, charcoal on beige paper, 12 x 16 7/8 in., 30.5 x 42.9 cm
Right: *Study for Jacob and the Angel,* 1931, charcoal on beige paper, 12 x 14 5/8 in., 30.5 x 37.2 cm

Woman Leaning on Hand, 1932, bronze, edition of 7, 6 x 7 1/4 x 7 3/4 in., 15.2 x 18.4 x 19.7 cm

Leaning on Head and Hands, 1932, bronze, edition of 7, 5 1/2 x 7 7/8 x 4 1/4 in., 13.9 x 20 x 10.8 cm

SELECTED SOLO EXHIBITIONS

1920 *Jacques Lipchitz*, Galerie de l'Effort Moderne, Paris.

1930 *Cent Sculptures par Jacques Lipchitz*, Galerie de la Renaissance, Paris, France.

1935-36 *Jacques Lipchitz*, Brummer Gallery, New York, New York, December 2-January 31.

1937 *Jacques Lipchitz*, at Les Maîtres de l'art indépendant, Paris World's Fair, Petit Palais, Paris, France.

1942 *Jacques Lipchitz*, Buchholz Gallery, New York, New York.

1943 *Jacques Lipchitz*, Buchholz Gallery, New York, New York.

1944 *The Drawings of Jacques Lipchitz*, Buchholz Gallery, New York, New York.

1946 *Jacques Lipchitz*, Buchholz Gallery, New York, New York.

Jacques Lipchitz, Galerie Maeght, Paris, France.

1948 *Jacques Lipchitz: Early Stone Carvings and Recent Bronzes*, Buchholz Gallery, New York, New York.

1950 *Jacques Lipchitz*, Petite Galerie du Séminaire, Brussels, Belgium.

1950-51 *Lipchitz: Works 1914-1950*, Portland Art Museum, Portland, Oregon; traveled to The San Francisco Museum of Art, San Francisco, California; The Cincinnati Art Museum, Cincinnati.

1951 *Jacques Lipchitz*, Buchholz Gallery, New York, New York.

Jacques Lipchitz: Birth of the Muses, The Museum of Modern Art, New York, New York.

1952 *Sculptura: Jacques Lipchitz*, French Pavilion, *XXVIth Biennale*, Venice, Italy, June 14-October 19.

Jacques Lipchitz, Frank Perls Gallery, Beverly Hills, California, and The Santa Barbara Museum of Art, Santa Barbara, California.

1954-55 *The Sculpture of Jacques Lipchitz*, The Museum of Modern Art, New York; traveled to Walker Art Center, Minneapolis, Minnesota; the Cleveland Museum of Art, Cleveland, Ohio.

1957 *Jacques Lipchitz: Thirty-Three Semi-Automatics, 1955-56 and Earlier Works, 1915-28*, Fine Arts Associates, New York, New York.

Jacques Lipchitz, Frank Perls Gallery, Beverly Hills, California.

Lipchitz: Small Sculptures, Cincinnati Art Museum, Cincinnati, Ohio.

1958-59 *Jacques Lipchitz*, Stedelijk Museum, Amsterdam; traveled to Rijksmuseum Kröller-Müller, Otterlo and elsewhere.

Jacques Lipchitz, École des Beaux-Arts, Montréal, Quebec; traveled in Canada to Norman MacKenzie Art Gallery, Regina, Saskatchewan and elsewhere.

Lipchitz, Städtische Galerie München, Munich, Germany.

1959 *Jacques Lipchitz*, Musée National d'Art Moderne, Paris, France.

Á La Limite du Possible, Jacques Lipchitz: Fourteen Recent Works, 1958-59, and Earlier Works, 1949-59, Fine Arts Associates, New York, New York.

Sculpture by Jacques Lipchitz, The Tate Gallery, London, England.

1960 *Juan Gris–Jacques Lipchitz: A Friendship*, M. Knoedler & Co., New York, New York.

Jacques Lipchitz: A Retrospective Exhibition of Sculpture and Drawings, The Corcoran Gallery, Washington, DC; traveled to Baltimore Museum of Art, Baltimore, Maryland.

1961-62 *Fifty Years of Lipchitz Sculpture*, Otto Gerson Gallery, New York, New York, November 7-December 9, 1961; traveled to Andrew Dickson White Museum of Art, Cornell University, Ithaca, New York.

1962 *Jacques Lipchitz: Recent Sculpture*, Otto Gerson Gallery, New York, New York.

1963-64 *Jacques Lipchitz: A Retrospective Selected by the Artist*, UCLA Art Galleries, University of California Art Council, Los Angeles, California; traveled to San Francisco Museum of Art, San Francisco, California and elsewhere.

1963-65 *Jacques Lipchitz: 157 Bronze Sketches 1912- 1962*, Otto Gerson Gallery, New York, New York; circulated by The Museum of Modern Art; traveled to Currier Gallery of Art, Manchester, New Hampshire and elsewhere in North and South America.

1964 *Jacques Lipchitz: Retrospective*, Boston University School of Fine and Applied Arts, Boston, Massachusetts.

Jacques Lipchitz, Marlborough-Gerson Gallery, New York, New York.

The Cubist Period of Jacques Lipchitz, The Phillips Collection, Washington, DC.

1964-65 *Between Heaven and Earth, Documenta International*, Kassel, June 27-October 5, and Carnegie International, Pittsburgh,Pennsylvania.

1965 *Jacques Lipchitz & Marc Chagall*, Israel Museum, Jerusalem.

Jacques Lipchitz, Newark Museum of Art, Newark, New Jersey.

1966 *Jacques Lipchitz: Images of Italy*, Marlborough- Gerson Gallery, New York, New York; traveled to Felix Landau Gallery, Los Angeles, California.

1967 *Jacques Lipchitz: Sculptures on Biblical Themes*, The Jewish Museum, New York, New York.

1968 *Lipchitz: The Cubist Period 1913-1930*, Marlborough-Gerson Gallery, New York, New York.

Jacques Lipchitz, Slosberg Art Gallery, Brandeis University, Waltham, Massachusetts.

1969 *The Sculpture of Jacques Lipchitz*, University of Wisconsin Art History Galleries, Milwaukee, Wisconsin; traveled to Herron Museum of Art, Indianapolis, Indiana.

Jacques Lipchitz, Katonah Gallery, Katonah, New York.

1970-71 *Jacques Lipchitz: Skulpturen und Zeichnugen 1911-1969*, Neue Nationalgalerie, Berlin; traveled to Staatliche Kunsthalle, Baden- Baden and elsewhere.

1971 *Jacques Lipchitz: Sculptures and Drawings 1911- 1970*, Tel Aviv Museum, Tel Aviv, Israel.

Jacques Lipchitz: Bronze Sketches, Israel Museum, Jerusalem, Israel.

1972 *Jacques Lipchitz: His Life in Sculpture*, The Metropolitan Museum of Art, New York, New York.

Jacques Lipchitz: Sculpture, Watercolors, and Drawings, Makler Gallery, Philadelphia, Pennsylvania.*Jacques Lipchitz*, Marlborough-Godard, Toronto, Ontario, Canada.

1973 *Jacques Lipchitz: Sculptures and Drawings*, Marlborough Fine Art, London; traveled as *Jacques Lipchitz: Skulpturen und Zeichnungen* to Marlborough Galerie, Zurich.

A Tribute to Jacques Lipchitz: Lipchitz in America, 1941-1973, Marlborough Gallery, New York, New York.

1974 *Sculptures by Jacques Lipchitz*, Brooks Memorial Art Gallery, Memphis, Tennessee.

Jacques Lipchitz: Sculptures, Prints, and Drawings, Baltimore Museum of Art, Baltimore, Maryland.

1974-75 *Selected Master Drawings of Jacques Lipchitz: 1910-1958*, Trisolini Gallery of Ohio University, Athens, Ohio; traveled to The Columbus Gallery of Fine Arts and elsewhere.

1977 *Jacques Lipchitz: Sculptures and Drawings from the Cubist Epoch*, Marlborough Gallery, New York, New York; traveled to Marlborough Galerie, Zurich and Marlborough Fine Art, London.

1978 *Oeuvres de Jacques Lipchitz (1891-1973)*, Musée National d'Art Moderne, Centre National d'Art et de Culture Georges Pompidou, Paris, France.

Jacques Lipchitz, Galerie Brusberg, Hannover, Germany.

1979 *Jacques Lipchitz: Small Sculptures, Maquettes and Drawings, 1915-1972*, Marlborough Gallery, New York, New York.

1981-82 *Jacques Lipchitz: Selected Sculpture in Large Scale 1927-1971*, Marlborough Gallery, New York, New York.

1982 *Jacques Lipchitz: Sculptures (Biblical Themes) 1930-1972*, Aberbach Fine Art, New York, New York.

1983 *Jacques Lipchitz: Mother and Child*, Norman Mackenzie Art Gallery, Univ. of Regina, Saskatchewan, Canada.

1985 *Jacques Lipchitz: Sculptor and Collector*, Albert and Vera List Visual Arts Center, Massachusetts Institute of Technology, Cambridge, Massachusetts.

Jacques Lipchitz: A Survey 1911-1973, Marlborough Fine Arts, Tokyo, Japan.

Jacques Lipchitz: Selected Sculpture, Reliefs & Drawings 1911-1972, Marlborough Gallery, New York, New York.

1986-87 *The Lipchitz Gift: Models for Sculpture*, The Tate Gallery, London, England.

1987 *Jacques Lipchitz: The Cubist Period (1913- 1930)*, Marlborough Gallery, New York.

1988 *Hommage à Lipchitz: œuvres de 1914 à 1963*, Galerie Marwan Hoss, Paris, France.

1989-90 *Jacques Lipchitz: A Life in Sculpture*, Art Gallery of Ontario, Toronto; traveled to Winnipeg Art Gallery, Winnipeg, Manitoba and elsewhere.

1991-92 *Jacques Lipchitz: From Sketch to Sculpture*, Tel Aviv Museum of Art, Tel Aviv, Israel.

1993 *Jacques Lipchitz: Esculturas, 1913-1972*, Galería Marlborough, Madrid, Spain

Jacques Lipchitz (1891-1973), Centro de Arte Palacio Almudi, Murcia..

1996 *Jacques Lipchitz: Sculpture 1910-1940*, The Paris Years, Marlborough Gallery, New York, New York.

Jacques Lipchitz, Galerie Gmurzynska, Marienburg, Germany.

1997 *Jacques Lipchitz, Escultura 1911-1971*, Marlborough Gallery, Madrid, Spain.

Lipchitz, un mundo sorprendido en el espacio, Museo Nacional Centro de Arte Reina Sofía, Madrid; traveled to Institut Valencià d'Art Modern, Centro Julio Gonzáles, Valencià, Spain.

1998 *Lipchitz dans les Jardins du Palais Royal*, Les Jardins du Palais Royal, Paris, France; traveled to Yorkshire Sculpture Park, Wakefield.

2001 *Lipchitz and the Avant-Garde: From Paris to New York*, Krannert Art Museum and Kinkead Pavilion, University of Illinois at Urbana-Champaign.

2002 *Los Dibujos de Lipchitz*, Institut Valencià d'Art Modern, Valencià, Spain.

Jacques Lipchitz: Drawing and Sculpture, Israel Museum, Jerusalem, Israel.

2003 *Jacques Lipchitz, Dibujos y Esculturas*, Museo de Bellas Artes de Bilbao, Bilbao, Spain.

2004 *Jacques Lipchitz: Sculpture and Drawings 1912 -1972*, Marlborough Gallery, New York,New York.

2005 *Jacques Lipchitz: Donation*, Museo de Bellas Artes de Bilbao, Bilbao, Spain.

Lipchitz: Les Années Françaises de 1910 à 1940, Musée de Années 30, Paris, France.

2006 *Jacques Lipchitz: Interación de Formas*, Fundación Bilbao Bizkaia Kutxa, Bilbao, Spain.

2007 *Jacques Lipchitz: Early Works, Reliefs and Drawings*, Marlborough Gallery, New York, New York.

Jacques Lipchitz – The American Years, Galerie Koch, Hannover, Germany.

2008 *Art Videos at the Gallery – Jacques Lipchitz: Portrait of the Artist*, Barn Gallery, Ogunquit, Maine.

Jacques Lipchitz. Sculptures – bas-reliefs et dessins, Marlborough Monaco, Monte Carlo, Monaco.

Encuentros, Jacques Lipchitz y el arte primitivo, Marlborough Barcelona, Barcelona, Spain.

2009 *Jacques Lipchitz. Dibujos*, Bilbao Bizkaia Kutxa, Bilbao, Spain.

Jacques Lipchitz Rétrospective. Le Bellevue, Biarritz, France.

The Anatomy of a Sculptor. Ben Uri Gallery, London, England.

2009-10 *Jacques Lipchitz: De la Joie de Vivre al Árbol de la Vida*, Museo de Navarra, Pamplona, Spain.

2010 *Jacques Lipchitz: Beyond Bible and Myth*, Marlborough Gallery, New York, New York.

Jacques Lipchitz: Obra Gráfica, Marlborough Gallery, Madrid, Spain.

2012 *Jacques Lipchitz: The Israel Museum Collection*, Museum Beelden aan Zee Scheveningen, Netherlands.

2013 *Jacques Lipchitz: Sculpture and Drawings*, Museo di Palazzo Pretorio, Prato, Italy.

2014 *Jacques Lipchitz: Retrospective*, Servizi Culturali, Locarno, Switzerland.

Jacques Lipchitz: Munich and Florence, Drawings for Sculpture 1910-1972, The Staatliche Graphische Sammlung, Munich, Germany; traveled to The Gabinetto Disegni e Stampe degli Uffizi, Florence, Italy.

2015 *Jacques Lipchitz: Selected Sculpture and Drawing from 1911 to 1972*, Marlborough Gallery, New York.

2017 *Jacques Lipchitz: Bildhauer des 20 Jahrhunderts*, Kunstsammlungen Chemnitz, Chemnitz, Germany.

2018 *Jacques Lipchitz (1891-1973): Retrospective*, Moscow Museum of Modern Art, Moscow, Russia (through 2019).

Selected Museum and Public Collections

Albright-Knox Art Gallery , Buffalo, New York
Art Gallery of Ontario, Toronto, Canada
Art Institute of Chicago, Chicago, Illinois
Baltimore Museum of Art, Baltimore, Maryland
Barnes Foundation, Philadelphia , Pennsylvania
Birmingham Museum of Art, Birmingham, Alabama
Broadgate, Broadgate Square, London , England
Bunkamura Museum of Art , Tokyo, Japan
Carnegie Museum of Art, Pittsburgh, Pennsylvania
Cleveland Museum of Art, Cleveland, Ohio
Contemporary Arts Museum, Houston, Texas
Dallas Museum of Art, Dallas, Texas
Davis Museum and Cultural Center, Wellesley College, Wellesley, Massachusetts
Denver Art Museum, Denver, Colorado
Des Moines Art Center, Des Moines, Iowa
Detroit Institute of Arts, Detroit, Michigan
Fogg Art Museum, Harvard University, Cambridge, Massachusetts
Galleria Nazionale d'Arte Moderna, Rome, Italy
Haags Gemeentemuseum, The Hague, Netherlands
Hakone Open-Air Museum , Hakone-machi, Japan
Hamburger Kunsthalle, Hamburg, Germany
Hirshhorn Museum and Sculpture Garden, Smithsonian Institution , Washington, D.C.
Honolulu Academy of Arts, Honolulu, Hawaii
Institut Valencià d'Art Modern (IVAM), Valencia, Spain
Israel Museum and Billy Rose Art Garden , Jerusalem , Israel
Kröller-Müller Museum, Otterlo, Netherlands
Kunsthaus Zürich, Zurich, Switzerland
Kunstmuseum Basel, Basel, Switzerland
Kunstmuseum Bern, Bern, Switzerland
Kunstmuseum Winterthur, Winterthur , Switzerland
Lille Métropole Musée d'Art Moderne , Villeneuve d'Ascq, France
Los Angeles County Museum of Art, Los Angeles, California
Milwaukee Art Museum, Milwaukee, Wisconsin
Minneapolis Institute of Arts, Minneapolis, Minnesota
Minnesota Museum of American Art, St. Paul, Minnesota
Miriam and Ira D. Wallach Art Gallery, Columbia University, New York, New York
Montréal Museum of Fine Arts, Montreal, Quebec, Canada
Museo Botero, Santafé de Bogotá, Colombia
Museo Nacional Centro de Arte Reina Sofía, Madrid, Spain
Museo de Arte de São Paulo Assis Chateaubriand, São Paulo, Brazil
Museo de Bellas Artes de Caracas, Caracas, Venezuela
Museu de Arte Moderna Rio de Janeiro, Rio de Janeiro, Brazil
Museum Boymans-van Beuningen, Rotterdam, Netherlands
Museum Folkwang, Essen, Germany
Museum Frieder Burda, Baden-Baden, Germany
Museum of Fine Arts, Houston, Texas
Musée National d'Art Moderne, Centre George Pompidou, Paris, France
Musée des Beaux-Arts, Nancy, France
Musée d'Art Moderne de la Ville de Paris, Paris, France
Musée d'Art Moderne et Contemporain, Strasbourg, France
Musée d'Art et d'Histoire du Judaïsme, Paris, France
National Gallery of Art, Washington, D.C.
National Gallery of Canada, Ottawa, Ontario , Canada
Nelson-Atkins Museum of Art, Kansas City, Missouri
New Orleans Museum of Art, New Orleans , Louisiana
Norton Museum of Art, West Palm Beach, Florida
Norton Simon Museum , Pasadena , California
Peggy Guggenheim Collection, Solomon R. Guggenheim Foundation, Venice, Italy
PepsiCo Sculpture Gardens , Purchase, New York
Philadelphia Museum of Art, Philadelphia , Pennsylvania
Phillips Collection, Washington, D.C.
Portland Art Museum, Portland, Oregon
Princeton University Art Museum, Princeton, New Jersey
Queensland Art Gallery , Brisbane, Australia
Saarland Museum, Saarbrücken, Germany
San Francisco Museum of Modern Art, San Francisco, California
Santa Barbara Museum of Art. Santa Barbara, California
Scottish National Gallery of Modern Art, Edinburgh, Scotland
Smith College Museum of Art, Northampton, Massachusetts
Sprengel Museum, Hannover, Germany
St. Louis Art Museum, Saint Louis, Missouri
Staatliche Kunsthalle, Karlsruhe, Germany
Staatsgalerie Stuttgart, Stuttgart, Germany
Stedelijk Museum, Amsterdam, Netherlands
Stedelijk Van Abbemuseum, Eindhoven, Netherlands
Städtische Kunsthalle Mannheim, Mannheim , Germany
Tate Britain, London, England
Tate Liverpool, Liverpool, England
Tate Modern, London, England
Tel Aviv Museum of Art, Tel Aviv, Israel
The Art Institute of Chicago, Chicago, Illinois
The Helena Rubinstein Pavilion for Contemporary Art, Tel Aviv, Israel
The Metropolitan Museum of Art, New York, New York
The Museum of Modern Art, New York, New York
The Solomon R. Guggenheim Museum, New York, New York
The State Hermitage Museum, St. Petersburg, Russia
Tokushima Modern Art Museum, Tokushima, Japan
Tweed Museum of Art, University of Minnesota Duluth, Duluth, Minnesota
UCLA Hammer Museum, University of California Los Angeles, Los Angeles, California
Virginia Museum of Fine Arts , Richmond, Virginia
Von der Heydt Museum, Wuppertal, Germany
Walker Art Center. Minneapolis, Minnesota
Whitney Museum of American Art, New York, New York
Worcester Art Museum, Worcester, Massachusetts

Marlborough

The Paris Years
is published on the occasion of
The Paris Years: Sculpture and Drawing, 1911-1932
Marlborough Gallery, New York
October 17–November 23, 2019

New York - Uptown
40 West 57th Street, #2
New York, NY 10019

New York - Downtown
545 West 25th Street
New York, NY 10001

London - Mayfair
6 Albemarle Street
London W1S 4BY

Cover:
Bather III, 1917
bronze, edition of 7
28 1/4 x 10 x 10 in.
71.8 x 25.4 x 25.4 cm

Back cover:
Pierrot, 1925
bronze, unique
7 3/4 x 4 1/2 x 2 1/2 in.
19.7 x 11.4 x 6.3 cm

Photo credits // Matt Grubb, Pierre Le Hors, Dennis Johnson, Bill Orcutt, & Reto Rodolfo Pedrini
Design // Brian Paul

ISBN: 978-089797516-2

Edition of 1200
Printed in New York by **PROJECT**